Rivers in American Life and Times

The Colorado River

The Columbia River

The Hudson River

The Mississippi River

The Missouri River

The Ohio River

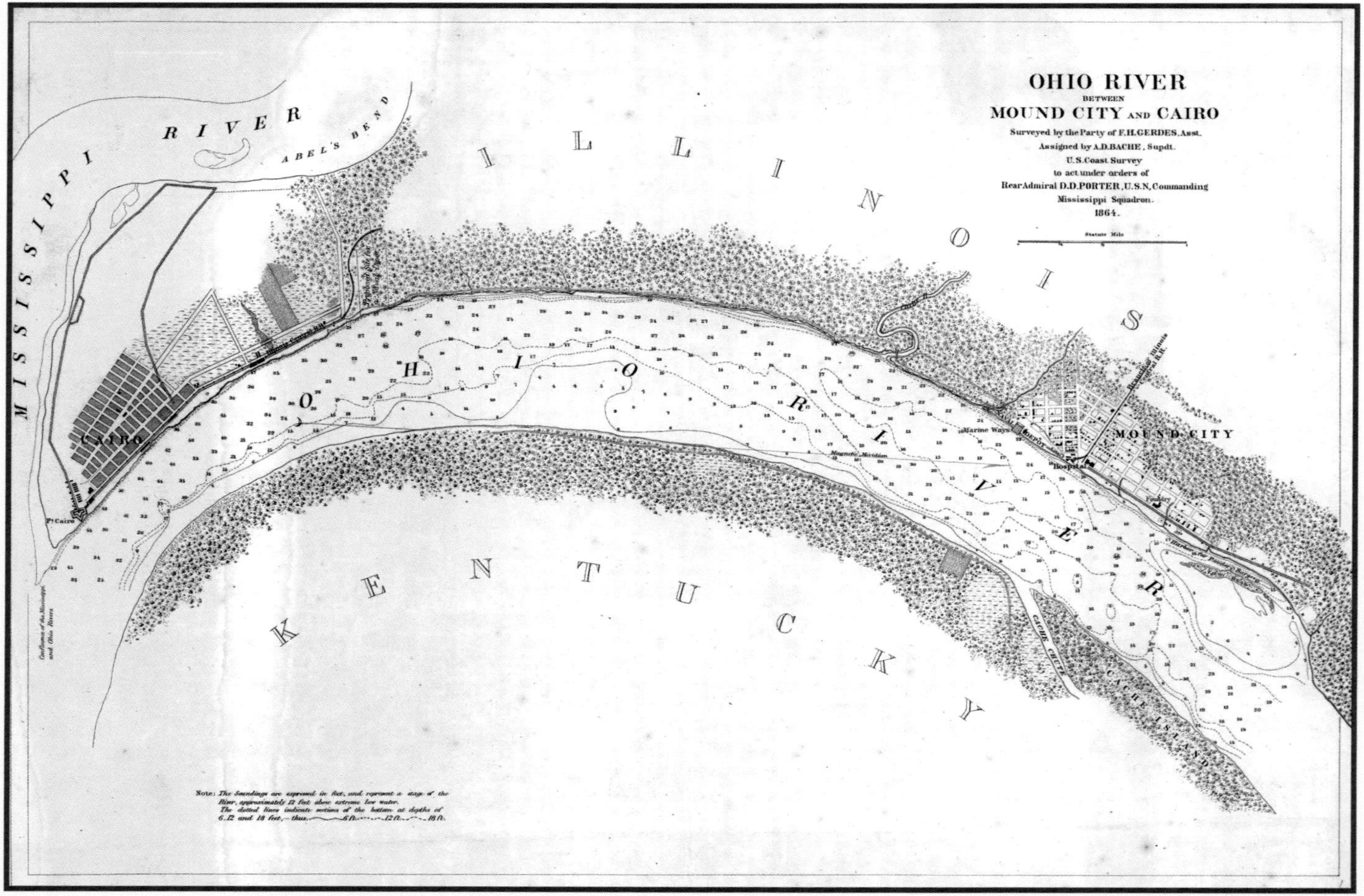
OHIO RIVER
BETWEEN
MOUND CITY AND CAIRO
Surveyed by the Party of F.H.GERDES, Asst.
Assigned by A.D.BACHE, Supdt.
U.S.Coast Survey
to act under orders of
Rear Admiral D.D.PORTER, U.S.N, Commanding
Mississippi Squadron.
1864.
Statute Mile
MISSISSIPPI RIVER
ABEL'S BEND
ILLINOIS
KENTUCKY
OHIO RIVER
CAIRO
Pt. Cairo
MOUND CITY
Marine Ways
Hospital
Magnetic Meridian
CACHE CHUTE
CACHE ISLAND
Confluence of the Mississippi and Ohio Rivers
Note: The Soundings are expressed in feet, and represent a stage of the River, approximately 12 feet above extreme low water.
The dotted lines indicate sections of the bottom at depths of 6, 12 and 18 feet, — thus, 6 ft. 12 ft. 18 ft.

RIVERS IN AMERICAN LIFE AND TIMES

THE OHIO RIVER

Tim McNeese

CHELSEA HOUSE PUBLISHERS
A Haights Cross Communications Company
Philadelphia

FRONTIS: Map of the Ohio River between Mound City and Cairo, Illinois.

CHELSEA HOUSE PUBLISHERS

VP, NEW PRODUCT DEVELOPMENT Sally Cheney
DIRECTOR OF PRODUCTION Kim Shinners
CREATIVE MANAGER Takeshi Takahashi
MANUFACTURING MANAGER Diann Grasse

Staff for THE OHIO RIVER

EXECUTIVE EDITOR Lee Marcott
PRODUCTION EDITOR Megan Emery
PHOTO EDITOR Sarah Bloom
SERIES DESIGNER Keith Trego
COVER DESIGNER Keith Trego
LAYOUT 21st Century Publishing and Communications, Inc.

A Haights Cross Communications Company

www.chelseahouse.com

First Printing

9 8 7 6 5 4 3 2 1

Library of Congress Cataloging-in-Publication Data

McNeese, Tim.
Ohio River / Tim McNeese.
v. cm. -- (Rivers in American life and times)
Includes index.
Contents: River origins and first peoples -- Exploring the Ohio -- Wars in the Ohio country
-- A prospect of commerce -- Days of steam and war
-- A river in transition -- The modern Ohio River.
ISBN 0-7910-7725-X-ISBN 0-7910-8008-0 (pbk.)
1. Ohio River--Description and travel--Juvenile literature. 2. Ohio River--History--Juvenile literature. [1. Ohio River.] I. Title. II. Series. F516.M34 2003 917.7--dc22
2003023917

Contents

1

River Origins and First Peoples

More than two centuries ago, President Thomas Jefferson referred to the Ohio as "the most beautiful river in the world." Today, the nearly 1,000 miles of the Ohio River remain one of the most heavily populated and industrialized river systems in America. Great barge cargoes laden with such industrial products as oil and steel slowly ply their way up and down the course of the river. Major cities, including Cincinnati, Ohio; Pittsburgh, Pennsylvania; and Louisville, Kentucky, dot both the northern and southern banks of the Ohio. Six states—Illinois, Indiana, Kentucky, Ohio, Pennsylvania, and West Virginia—share the Ohio River. During the late 1700s and early 1800s, the Ohio River became the border for five of those six states. Kentucky lays claim to the longest stretch of the Ohio: Hundreds of miles of the river form that state's northern and western border.

The modern-day Ohio measures approximately 981 miles in length and is a river fed by dozens of tributaries, including extensive river systems. More than 5,000 miles of major river channels feed into the Ohio, including such important inland waterways as the Allegheny and Monongahela Rivers, which form the Ohio's headwaters, and the Muskingum, Little Kanawha, Hocking, Scioto, Licking, Great Miami, Kentucky, Salt, Green Wabash, Tradewater, Cumberland, and Tennessee Rivers.

The river has always been a fascinating and vital resource for all populations that have lived along its banks, fished its waters, tapped its natural resources, and otherwise utilized the river as a major transportation route through the interior of North America. From the time of its earliest inhabitants, the Ohio River has boasted an alluring environment:

> To the Indians, *O-hi-o* meant "Beautiful River," and the French called it precisely that, "La Belle Rivière." With hill-framed loops and bends and noble vistas, the river led through a green wilderness. There were bold hills, long forest slopes, rich benchlands of wood and meadow. In spring redbud and dogwood lighted the underforest; in fall the pale

> sycamores shown through the russet of beech groves and the gold of hickory. The woods were alive with birds of many colors—scarlet cardinals, white-barred blue jays, green and yellow parakeets. Every fall the skies darkened with clouds of passenger pigeons.[1]

For thousands of years, the Ohio River has served as a magnet for human occupation. Countless generations of North America's first inhabitants, the Native Americans or Indians, lived along its banks, sharing the river with teeming populations of wildlife, including deer, elk, bears, and, in more remote times, woolly mammoths and long-tusked mastodons. In more recent centuries, the Ohio River and its 1,000-mile-long valley has provided an organic center stage for voyages of discovery, battles of war, settlements of progress, and the development of industry. The region of the Ohio saw some of the first white settlers to cross the Appalachian Mountains from the British colonies of the Atlantic seaboard. Romantic eras of keelboats and paddle-wheeled steamers created indelible scenes of western frontier movement and pioneer commerce. The river became a line of demarcation between the slaveholding states of the American South and the free states of the American Union. The river has lain witness to misuse and abandon, economic stagnation and political division, and the drama of humanity and the rage of nature's flooding. In the words of historian Betty Bryant, "The Ohio River Valley has a rich story to tell, in and of itself as a fascinating geologic, geographic entity and through diverse waves of inhabitants whose known residency spans from the withdrawal of the last great glaciers some 15,000 years ago up to the present."[2]

Most of the modern-day Ohio River is not an ancient waterway, not when compared to other rivers, including those of North America. The river that cuts its course in a southwesterly direction from Pittsburgh, Pennsylvania, to Cairo, Illinois, is perhaps no more than several tens of thousands of years old. Long before the Ohio River was created, much of the North

American continent was covered by water, forming a vast interior sea. This great sea teemed with prehistoric life, including "octopuslike creatures, sluggish giant snails or gastropods fifteen feet long."[3] Modern geologists call this extensive inland body of water "Lake Ohio." This saltwater lake measured at least 400 miles in length and 200 miles across. It covered the site of modern-day Pittsburgh with water 300 feet deep.

During this period, much of the bedrock that lies beneath the Ohio Valley today was established. In time, the sea became a vast frozen wasteland as the North American continent experienced a prolonged ice age. Glaciers a mile thick covered the lands and cut jagged trenches for water routes. The recurring periods of massive glaciers that covered the Ohio River basin for hundreds of miles—geologists count as many as six different glacial ages that spread ice across the Ohio Valley—shaped the landscape. As successive glaciers moved and shifted, they formed the topography of the Ohio Valley, creating low courses for rivers and low-lying mountains.

These same glaciers created river courses, including the early tributaries of the Ohio—the Monongahela and the Allegheny Rivers. Although the Ohio Valley would experience thousands of years more of geological change, the basic course of the modern-day Monongahela already had been established.

Much of this early river formation was determined by the extent and distribution of the region's vast glacial formations. By the end of the most recent ice age, the modern-day Ohio was about to take shape. In his book *Rivers of America: The Ohio*, historian R.E. Banta noted this transformation:

> By the time the cycle of cold weather was over and the icecap finally retreated forever . . . the present drainage was established. The Kanawha, Sandy, Kentucky, Green, Cumberland, and Tennessee flowed north into the new Ohio through their old courses and new, or partly new, rivers came down from the north to add their waters. The Ohio system as we know it was established.[4]

For thousands of years to follow, the old glaciers melted, reshaping the land, leaving the region frozen for several months of each passing year. Even in the midst of summer, the rivers of the Ohio Valley continued to run ice cold. As the average temperature of the region continued to warm, the contrast of the remaining ice caused an air temperature that was chilly and also a nearly year-round fog.

In this open-refrigerator environment, the Ohio Valley was dotted with warm zones, where underground springs reached the earth's surface. Such locales became grounds for grasses and plants that provided food for the Pleistocene animals of the last ice age. The springs brought salt deposits, left behind from the evaporation of the great inland sea that had once covered the region, to the surface as well. These warm-spring valleys

> became the haunt of a varied and exotic animal life, examples of which were preserved for the amazement of modern man in that natural pickling vat, the Big Bone Lick, which lay a short distance from the Ohio River in present north central Kentucky. Mastodon, arctic elephant, peccary, giant elk—the bones of all those and probably also of tapir and giant sloth were still strewn about the lick in historic times. Animals and reptiles even earlier extinct had also visited the place occasionally.[5]

As these animals gathered near these prehistoric sources of salt and warmth, human beings eventually caught up with them.

Exactly when the first humans reached the region of the Ohio Valley remains a subject of controversy. Modern anthropologists continue to push the date back to earlier millennia with each new discovery of early human habitation. For most experts, an acceptable arrival date in the region lies between 10,000 and 20,000 years ago. These early humans lived in the pine and hardwood forests of the Great Lakes and the Ohio Valley and used stone tools and weapons, such as axes and adzes. They used such tools to carve dugout canoes from complete tree trunks. Their stone tools have been uncovered at sites along the Licking River, which runs diagonally across modern-day Kentucky until it reaches the Ohio River near Cincinnati, and at Golconda, Illinois, near where the Ohio River dumps into the Mississippi River.

By 5000 B.C., these First Peoples of the Ohio were working with copper, creating spearheads, axes, knives, awls, and wedges for splitting tree trunks. They also hammered raw copper into decorative items, such as bracelets and other trinkets. These early arrivals were hunting societies, nomadic peoples who tracked the big game of the period using stone-tipped spears.

The oldest known occupants of the Ohio River Valley to remain in the region and establish a continuous history of settlement were those peoples archaeologists call the Mound Builders. Mound building was practiced by multiple native culture groups dating back several thousand years. The earliest Mound Builders raised their earthen works as early as 2,500 years ago. Archaeologists call these earliest Mound Builders the Adena, after a region in the state of Ohio where some of the oldest mounds were discovered. The Adena built their mounds for several purposes, the most important of which was to serve as burial sites for their dead. Some of these early mounds were cone-shaped, and others were constructed in the shapes of animals, including frogs, bears, and birds.

The next significant group of Mound Builders was those of the Hopewellian Culture. The Hopewellian Era began as early as 2,000 years ago and flourished from A.D. 500 to 700. The Hopewell Culture produced mounds on a grander scale than the Adena peoples had. Their mounds were larger, and the artifacts unearthed by archaeologists in these later mounds reveal a culture that was generally wealthier, traded on a greater scale geographically, and included larger population groups than the Adena.

Between 1000 and 1600, the occupants of the Ohio River Valley developed into modern tribes that were in place by the arrival of the first Europeans to the region. The tribes located in

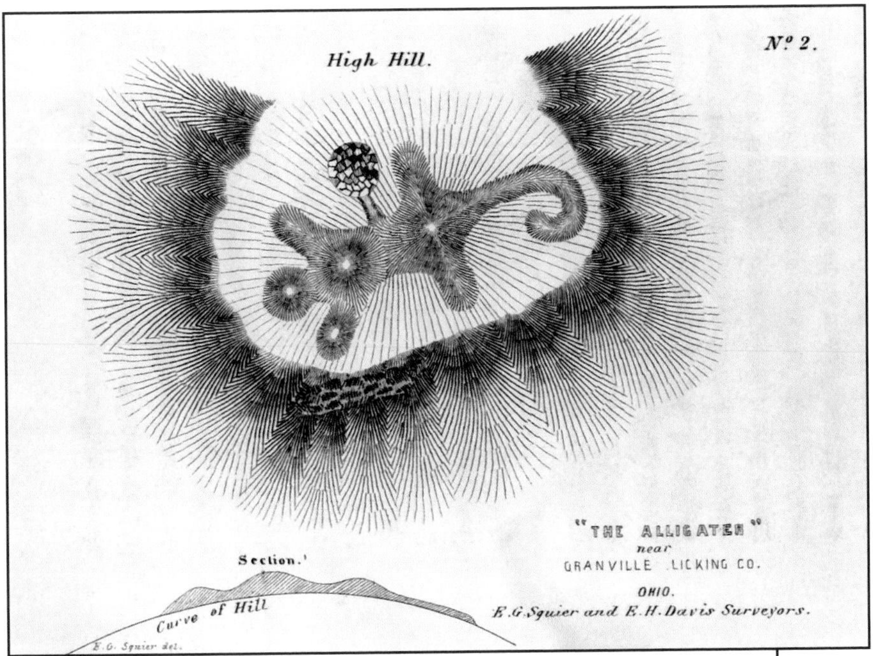

The first inhabitants of the Ohio River Valley were the Mound Builders, native culture groups that created mounds for several purposes, including burial sites. The mounds were often shaped as animals, like this alligator-shaped burial mound in Ohio.

southern Wisconsin and Ohio developed from the Hopewellian Culture into the Effigy Mound Culture. This culture era was noted for the burial sites the natives constructed in the shapes of animals and birds. In southwestern Ohio, the Indians constructed one of the more famous of the effigy mounds, the Great Serpent Mound.

Contemporaries of the Effigy Mound Culture, a regional group that anthropologists call the Middle Mississippi Culture, lived along the Ohio River, and some of their descendents remained in the region until the time of the arrival of the first Europeans. They, too, were mound builders, erecting their great earthen pyramids, such as the Cahokia Mound near St. Louis, and the Angel Mounds Site, near present-day Evansville, Indiana.

THE MYSTERIOUS MOUNDS OF THE OHIO COUNTRY

As Native American culture groups abandoned their settlements in the Ohio Country in the 1700s, they left behind intriguing remnants of their various mound building cultures: the mounds themselves. As European and American explorers and other frontier advancemen arrived in the region, they found such mounds fascinating, mysterious, and inviting.

The first non-Indian known to have discovered the largest mound near Moundsville, known today as the Grave Creek Mound, was an Ohio Valley pioneer named Joseph Tomlinson who, in 1770, actually walked off the top of the mound while out on a hunting foray. In 1772, the great American frontiersman George Rogers Clark camped near modern-day Moundsville, West Virginia, on the Upper Ohio River, "in the shadow of the great mound, 90 feet high, 300 paces around, 50 feet across the top."* Although the mound intrigued him, he did not examine the site, but could only wonder what the Native Americans, who had long abandoned it, had used the mound for.

In 1803, Reverend Thaddeus Mason Harris, an American minister, traveled from Massachusetts out to the frontier in an effort to recover from a serious bout of yellow fever. When he reached the Moundsville region, he discovered nine mounds at Grave Creek, all scattered along the banks of the Ohio. A local resident had dug into one of the mysterious mounds while making an icehouse, only to discover, according to Harris, "a vast number of human bones, a variety of stone tools, and a stone signet of an oval shape."** Harris examined the remaining mounds, including the largest of the nine, which the minister believed

These natives also erected around their villages fort walls of standing posts bound together with woven vines.

Agriculture was an important part of the economic life of the Ohio Valley Mississippians. They grew crops of corn, beans, and squash—called the Three Sisters by many Native Americans—as well as tobacco, flax, and hemp. They hunted using bows and arrows as well as spears. Hand axes were also in use, and the Mississippians caught animals in nets and traps. Their potters produced excellent samples of pottery, including clay models, or effigies, of animals, birds, and men. Their handicrafts included leather working and basketry. They were highly skilled weavers, probably held many intriguing items. Through his examinations, he noted in his journal that "the mound sounds hollow."*** Harris never dug into the great mound.

Another 35 years passed before the large mound was excavated. In 1838, a pair of amateur archaeologists, Jesse Tomlinson and Thomas Briggs, came to the mound and began digging. After several weeks of excavating at the base of the mound, they hit on a burial chamber, which contained a pair of skeletons and hundreds of ivory beads. As they dug near the top of the mound, the curious excavators unearthed additional skeletons. Another burial find uncovered yet another skeleton "adorned with 1,700 ivory beads, 500 seashells, and 5 copper bracelets."+ Tomlinson and Briggs basically looted the site of its treasures while destroying much of the archaeological evidence. Later, Tomlinson (a descendent of Joseph Tomlinson) opened the mound as a tourist attraction, charging 25 cents for entrance into Grave Creek Mound's center chamber.

The mound faced repeated abuse during the following years, as it was used as a saloon, dance platform, and as the site of an artillery battery during the Civil War. The Grave Creek Mound was not examined by a trained archaeologist until 1975, when Dr. E. Thomas Hemmings conducted the first scientific excavation at the site. The mound is now part of Grave Creek Mound State Park.

* Quoted in Havighurst, *River to the West,* 15.

** Ibid., 16.

*** Ibid.

\+ Ibid.

producing elaborate garments, including sandals and robes covered with feathers. Their artisans fashioned both functional and decorative items from copper, bone, wood, and stone.

Many of the mound-building cultures of the Ohio River Valley vanished over time, long before the arrival of Europeans to the region. Some of them moved south and joined with other mound building groups, such as the Choctaw, Chickasaw, Cherokee, and Natchez. Sometimes, the Mississippians were pushed out of the Ohio Country by tribes moving down from the north. Some Indians did remain along the banks of the Ohio River. The Piankishaw, as well as a small number of Illini and Kaskaskia, continued in their river settlements in southern Illinois and Indiana.

As Europeans established colonies along the Atlantic Coast and in modern-day Canada, northeastern tribes were pushed west and south, forcing them into the Ohio Valley. The Iroquois, native to modern-day New York, were pushed south into the upper Ohio River region and, in turn, pushed others out. A general evacuation of the lands south of the Ohio River resulted in Kentucky's becoming a land of few permanent occupants. Instead, the central region of Kentucky, lands that came to be known as the Blue Grass Region, became hunting grounds, neutral territory for many tribes. With a limited number of occupants in the region, the Ohio River Country became, by the 1700s, an inviting destination for non-Indians, both Europeans and Americans. As whites moved west across the Appalachian Mountains and down from Canada through the Great Lakes, the future of the Ohio River changed forever.

2

Exploring the Ohio

During the seventeenth century, the North American continent became the scene of repeated colonization efforts by various European powers. The French established a vast colony in modern-day Canada, which they called New France. One by one, English colonizers sailed across the Atlantic and established British colonies along the eastern seaboard, from New England to Virginia to Georgia. Others—the Dutch, the Swedes, the Finns—reached out to the New World with hopes of making their presence permanent. As more and more Europeans landed in North America, they began to fan out, searching for new locales for their settlements, their missions, their trading posts, and their homes and farms. As they explored the vast North American continent, they finally reached into the interior and made the European discovery of the Ohio River, a waterway the Native Americans had reached thousands of years earlier.

By the mid-1600s, Europeans had heard repeated stories of a great river that flowed to the southwest until it reached saltwater. Many European explorers hoped the river might prove to be the elusive (and nonexistent) Northwest Passage, a water route leading through the American continent to the Pacific Ocean. As a result, several Europeans went in search of the river west of the Appalachians and south of the Great Lakes. One of the earliest to record information about the Ohio River was a French Jesuit priest, Father Lalemant. Writing from Montreal in 1662, Lalemant related information about a party of Iroquois who had raided to the west in search of slaves. Lalemant wrote of the river, "Their villages are situated along a Beautiful River, which serves to carry people down to the Great Lake (for so they call the sea), where they trade with Europeans who pray as we do. From their account, we suppose these Europeans to be Spaniards."[6] Father Lalemant believed that this fabled river flowed to the Pacific Ocean. He did not realize that the Ohio flowed into the Mississippi River, which reaches the waters of the Gulf of Mexico.

The following year, French authorities in New France sent gentlemen explorers in search of not only the Ohio River but also of the Mississippi and several other rivers. Typically, such explorers attached themselves to Native American guides who knew the countryside and could often lead them directly to their destinations. One of the most successful of these explorers was a Frenchman named René-Robert Cavelier, Sieur de La Salle, an aristocrat who earlier had studied to become a Jesuit priest. He arrived in New France in 1667. After his arrival, he may have learned of Father Lalemant's writings and, after making inquiries with local Indians, he received permission to explore to the southwest of Montreal. With money raised by selling and mortgaging his land holdings in the New World, La Salle outfitted his expedition, purchasing four large canoes and employing 14 voyageurs, or French boatmen. French priests were later added to the party, and the number of boats increased to seven. The party was led by a canoe of Native Americans, Seneca warriors who served as guides. The Seneca knew of the Ohio, a river they called the "Oyo."

La Salle's party set out in 1669 in search of the Ohio River, which the French aristocrat hoped would lead his group to a direct route to China. From Montreal, the explorers, boatmen, and missionaries traveled more than a month until they reached a Seneca village near Lake Ontario, having covered 300 miles of territory. Here, the Frenchmen met with the local Seneca, who provided them with further information about the location of the Ohio River they were searching for. La Salle was informed that the river was another 360 miles away. The Frenchmen continued, paddling their canoes along the south banks of Lake Ontario, passing the Niagara River, until they arrived at the lake's westernmost shores. They camped again at another Indian village and purchased a pair of Native American slaves who told the Frenchmen that they knew of the river's location. After another two days of travel, they reached an Ottawa village, where they made contact with a Frenchman

One of the most successful explorers sent to chart the rivers of North America was Frenchman Robert Cavelier, Sieur de La Salle. Although some historians debate whether La Salle actually found the Ohio River, French claims to the region along the Ohio River near the Great Lakes were based on his explorations.

named Louis Joliet, another explorer, who was looking for a fabled copper mine in the Great Lakes Region. La Salle learned more from Joliet and, after several days of rest, continued. Two of his priests abandoned him at this juncture, after Joliet informed them of a group of Potawatomi Indians in the area of Lake Superior who might make good Christian converts. The party proceeded along Lake Erie to the Allegheny River, which led them directly to the Ohio River. Although there is some modern controversy concerning whether La Salle actually reached the Ohio itself, a French claim to the region was later based on the explorations of the aristocratic Frenchman. (Joliet made his own historical legacy during the early 1670s when he and a French Jesuit named Father Jacques Marquette became the first Frenchmen of record to reach the Upper Mississippi River.)

Even if La Salle did manage to reach the waters of the Upper Ohio, he may not have been the first European to do so. The British, operating from their colonies on the Atlantic Coast, also went in search of the Ohio during the seventeenth century. Between 1654 and 1664, an English fur trader, Abraham Woods, claimed to have reached several tributary rivers of the Ohio. Again, there are historical doubts about whether Woods actually accomplished what he claimed. Other British discoveries of the Ohio probably predated Woods's efforts, however, because British traders and trappers regularly traveled up the rivers of Virginia and New York and probably would have found their way to the Ohio's eastern banks. In the end, the exact European discovery of the Ohio River remains mysterious and controversial.

One of the best indicators of European knowledge of the Ohio comes from the published maps of the seventeenth century. After Marquette and Joliet's explorations of the Mississippi, the mouth of the Ohio began appearing on maps. Such maps "were showing the lower Ohio with fair accuracy but the upper Ohio remained a blank for decades to come."[7] By 1684, maps published in Paris included the Ohio under a variety of names, including Fleuve St. Louis, ou Chucagoa, and ou Casquinampogamou. By 1684, Marquette and Joliet, while exploring the Mississippi, had paddled their canoes past the mouth of the Ohio. La Salle himself, in the early 1680s, had reached the mouth of the Ohio while floating the Mississippi, following that great river all the way to the Gulf of Mexico.

Ironically, later maps, those published during the next 40 years, seem to have lost the river altogether. In 1720, the river was picked up again, this time by Alexander Spotswood, a governor of Virginia, who explored the western reaches of his commonwealth. On the map he drew of his discoveries, which he sent to London, he included a river he called the "Oubache River" (probably the Wabash River) and an elongated river he labeled the "Coosati River," which flowed west from the Appalachians. With these two rivers, Spotswood was probably trying to include the Ohio River on his map.

In time, the French became less interested in the Ohio River, especially after their discovery of the Mississippi River in the 1670s. The river remained important, however, to the British, especially those living in Virginia. The Virginians believed that their colony continued beyond the Appalachians, and they were interested in a river that flowed to the west. In 1729, Virginian William Byrd referred to the Ohio in his writing when he stated, "the sources of Potomac, Roanoke and even of the Shenandoah are unknown to the Virginian authorities; although woodsmen tell them they head in the same mounts with a branch of the Mississippi [the Ohio River]."[8]

The Upper Ohio remained vague and misplaced, even missing, from maps for several years, until the 1690s, when a Dutchman from Albany, New York, explored the river. Arnout Viele previously had served as an interpreter to the Iroquois of New York, serving various Albany traders. After going into business for himself, Viele made contact with several Shawnee natives. He decided to visit the lands of the Shawnee, which, at that time, were located south of the Ohio River in Kentucky. In the fall of 1692, he set out with 11 other white men and a handful of Mohawk and Shawnee. The mixed party traveled across western Pennsylvania, following the Wyoming Valley. They reached the Susquehanna River and the Allegheny River, which led them to the Ohio. Over several months, Viele's party paddled the full length of the Ohio River, to the river's mouth, where they remained through the spring of 1694. In time, after having established further trading connections with the Shawnee, Viele returned from his extensive trade explorations. Although no extensive British expansion into the Ohio Valley followed Viele's explorations, his voyage down the Ohio became well known. It was even written of by the founder of the French colony of Louisiana, Pierre Le Moyne d'Iberville during the late 1690s: "I am well aware that some men, twelve in number, and some Maheingans—started seven years ago from New York, in order to ascend the River Andaste Susquehanna, in the Province of Pennsylvania, as far as the River Ohio, which is said to join the Oubache, emptying together into the Mississippi. . . ."[9]

Viele's explorations were soon followed by those of a party from the British colonies, this one involving English traders from Charleston, South Carolina. This group set out in 1700 for the Ohio Country, taking along with them a French guide, Jean Coutoure, who had served La Salle during the 1680s on the Lower Mississippi River, until La Salle was murdered by disgruntled colonists. Now in the service of British traders, Coutoure led them into the Ohio interior, down the Tennessee River to the Ohio River, then the Mississippi, to the Arkansas, where they established a British trading post. (Ironically, it was here that Coutoure previously had served as commander of a French outpost.) For 12 years, this British outpost engaged in regular trade with the Indians in the region, until the French drove them out.

Throughout the eighteenth century, Europeans, especially the British and French, explored, paddled, and mapped the Ohio River. Yet during the hundred years from 1650 until the clash of arms between the French and British called the French and Indian War, the region went largely unnoticed by the British government in London and the French government in Paris. Even provincial capitals in North America—Montreal, Quebec, Albany, Williamsburg, Charleston—only recognized the region for its trade potential, not as a place for extensive settlement. The river itself was no longer a waterway of

THE SHAWNEE: PEOPLE OF THE OHIO COUNTRY

No discussion of the Ohio River during the seventeenth, eighteenth, and nineteenth centuries can fail to include one of the most significant and powerful nations of Native Americans—the Shawnee. They were a people who gained a reputation on the Ohio frontier for their ruthlessness, shrewd diplomacy, and ability to cooperate with their neighbors when it served their purposes.

They were known by the Iroquois as the *Ontouagannaha*, meaning "the people who speak an unknown language." The Shawnee called themselves the *sa wanna,* "the people of the South." For hundreds of years, the Shawnee people may have wandered over a great expanse of North America, from Labrador in Canada to modern-day South Carolina. It appears that in 1614, the larger part of the Shawnee was living along the banks of the Delaware River, along the border region between Pennsylvania and New Jersey. While living there, the Shawnee lived alongside the Quaker colonists of Pennsylvania in peace. In 1736, however, Pennsylvania "granted the Iroquois hegemony over all other tribes in the colony because of their military power."* In time, the Iroquois of New York were pushing the Shawnee out of the region to the west, toward the Ohio Country beyond the Appalachian Mountains.

Despite such harassment from the Iroquois, the Shawnee remained in the Ohio Valley throughout the eighteenth century and became one of the dominant tribes in the region.

Their reputation as fighters was well known, and they came to symbolize

mystery, a westerly flowing stream unmarked on any European's map. As historian R.E. Banta noted:

> By 1700, then, the Ohio—La Belle Rivière of the French—was fairly well known in its lower reaches, say below the mouth of the Great Miami [near modern-day Lawrenceburg, Indiana]. Arnout Viele, the Albany Dutchman, had traded upon it; La Salle's canoes had traversed it, from the Wabash down . . . before 1688; Coutour had led a party to and down a part of it. The upper half of the river had been navigated twice by Viele's men, perhaps once in full and once in small part by La Salle's,

the style of warfare that became commonplace in the region. In a 1755 fight with British regular troops, the Redcoats, the Shawnee captured several prisoners. These hapless victims were stripped, tortured, scalped, and burned. One eyewitness noted one prisoner's agonizing ordeal at the hands of the Shawnee:

> The prisoner was tied to the stake with his hands raised above his head, stripped naked, and surrounded by Indians. They would touch him with redhot irons, and stick his body full of pine splinters and set them on fire—drowning the shrieks of the victim in the yells of delight with which they danced around him.**

The Shawnee remained a force to be reckoned with into the nineteenth century even as non-Indian migration continued to deliver thousands of pioneers into the trans-Appalachian region of Ohio, Indiana, and Kentucky. Despite the singular efforts of such Shawnee leaders as Tecumseh and others, by the early decades of the 1800s, the Shawnee had been completely removed from their traditional lands in the Ohio Country.

* Quoted in R. Douglas Hurt, *The Ohio Frontier: Crucible of the Old Northwest, 1720–1830* (Bloomington: Indiana University Press, 1996), 10.

** Quoted in Banta, 93.

> and possibly by others. This upper half was known, surely, but it was still unmapped and thus far largely disregarded officially by both French and British.[10]

Yet for all the official disregard of both European governments abroad during the first half of the eighteenth century, by the 1750s, these two important powers would engage in a war over the Ohio Country, a conflict of global proportions.

3

Wars in the Ohio Country

The British colonists had remained largely along the Atlantic seaboard during the 1600s, but by the 1700s, more and more of them were moving west. Some established trade connections west of the Appalachians, and others were intent on claiming western lands and staking a permanent claim where they could build a pioneer cabin and farm. By the 1750s, France and England were at odds with each other over a significant portion of this highly prized western territory: the Ohio River Country.

The French in New France, to the north, had established a more permanent settlement pattern north of the Ohio River by the early decades of the eighteenth century. They had erected a string of military and trading posts throughout the Great Lakes Region stretching to the mouth of the Ohio, where the river flowed into the Mississippi. On the Illinois side of the Mississippi, near modern-day St. Louis, Cahokia had been established in 1699. Four years later, another fort—Kaskaskia—was built just seven miles away. Other forts, including Detroit (1701), Post Vincennes (by the late 1690s), and Post Ouiatenon (1717), on the Wabash River, near the mouth of the Tippecanoe River, were also constructed. By mid-eighteenth century, the French constructed Fort Presque Isle along the southern shore of Lake Erie, followed by Fort Le Boeuf, southwest of Presque Isle. In 1754, they built Fort Verango on the Allegheny, a tributary of the Ohio River. These forts and others built by the French served as a clear wake-up call to the British that the French were intent on claiming and occupying the rich lands of the Ohio Country.

During these same years, the British secured their claims on the Ohio Country by other means. In 1744, a group of delegates representing New York, Pennsylvania, Maryland, and Virginia met in the frontier town of Lancaster, Pennsylvania, to purchase a tract of the Ohio Country from the dominant tribe in the region, the Iroquois. It was the land sale (the Iroquois were given large quantities of rum before agreeing to the land transfer) that the British used to justify their claims to the upper region of the Ohio River. A few years later, the British took another decisive step into the Ohio Country. A land speculation company called the Ohio Company of Virginia was formed in 1747 and received a royal charter two years later, as well as a grant of a half million acres of Ohio land that spread along both the northern and southern banks of the Ohio River. In forming the company, its proprietors stated that one of their goals was "to anticipate the French by taking possession of that country southward to the Lakes to which the French have no right."[11]

In exchange for this generous grant of prime western lands, the Ohio Company agreed to move and settle 300 colonial families along the Ohio and erect two forts for their protection. One fort was to be built at the mouth of the Kanawha and the other at the source of the Ohio, where the Monongahela and Allegheny Rivers met in western Pennsylvania.

In direct response, the governor of New France dispatched a French military unit, under the command of Pierre Joseph de Celoron de Bienville (sometimes spelled "Blainville") into the Ohio Country in 1749. His orders were to make the French claim to the Ohio region clear to all he encountered there and to meet with Native American tribal leaders and attempt to either create alliances or inform them they must leave "French soil." Celoron set out for the frontier region with over 200 men, including soldiers, priests, hunters, guides, and boatmen.

Along the way, Celoron nailed plates bearing the royal arms of the king of France to trees and buried lead plates along the banks of the Ohio "as a token of renewal of possession heretofore taken of the aforesaid River Ohio, of all streams that fall into it, and all lands on both sides of the source of the aforesaid streams."[12] Celoron continued his march to the Great Miami (near modern-day Lawrenceburg, Indiana), which he followed north, where he met with the Miami Indians. He offered them good trade terms and encouraged them not to trade with the British. Despite Celoron's best efforts to deliver a clear message of French ownership of the Ohio Country, his impressive flags, his fancy uniforms, and his display of weapons did little to change the minds and loyalties of the Indians in the Ohio Country. When he finally returned north to New France, he wrote, "All I can say is, that the tribes of these localties are very badly disposed toward the French and entirely devoted to the English."[13]

Despite Celoron's mission, plans continued for the Ohio Company's opening of the Ohio Country. Access into the region first had to be improved, and a colonist named Thomas Cresap was employed to open up a road from Cumberland, Maryland, through the Appalachian range to the Monongahela River. (The basic route established by Cresap later became known as Braddock's Road, after a British general who marched an army into the region in 1755.) The company also employed Christopher Gist, a surveyor, to "go . . . to the Westward of the [Appalachians] . . . to Search out and discover Lands upon the river Ohio. . . . When you find a large quantity of good, level Land, such as you think will suit the Company, You are to measure the Breadth of it."[14] Gist was also ordered by Virginia's governor, Robert Dinwiddie, to negotiate with any local tribes to provide their support against the French. Celoron had entered the Ohio River Country with more than 200 men, but Gist set out across the Appalachians with one black slave. For the next two years, Gist surveyed, met with various Indian tribes, and meticulously explored the Ohio region. For much of his time in the Ohio Country, Gist had to operate quietly, secretively, because the region was teeming with French traders and agents intent on eliminating the English presence.

As Gist carried out his mission of negotiating, surveying, and exploring the Ohio River Country, other whites were also staking a claim to the region. An Irish-born trader, John Finley, reached the blue grass region south of the Ohio in central Kentucky by the early 1750s. A few years later, Finley spoke of his explorations in the lands south of the Ohio, describing the region as a great hunters' paradise, a place thick with wild game, including buffalo, deer, elk, bears, and turkeys, which Finley claimed were so numerous they could not all take flight simultaneously without darkening the sky. One of those who heard of Kentucky from Finley was a young North Carolinian named Daniel Boone. Perhaps one of the greatest of the trans-Appalachian frontiersmen, Boone would lead a group of Kentucky colonists into the blue grass region south of the Ohio River by the late 1760s.

Gist, after his return from his early 1750s reconnaissance in the Ohio River Country, was hired by Governor Dinwiddie in November 1753 to lead a Virginia militia major into the upper Ohio Country wilderness to deliver a message to the French commandant at Fort Le Boeuf. The militia major was none other than George Washington. Although the message, one that demanded that the French evacuate the Ohio region, was delivered, Washington and Gist's mission did not yield positive results. The French remained intent on controlling the Ohio Country, and, in the spring of 1754, carried out a raid against the Ohio Company's unfinished fort near the Forks of the Ohio River. In January 1755, the French "made an offer of compromise upon the control of the Ohio country but official England . . . refused to accept."[15] War between the two stubborn European powers soon engulfed the British colonies and the Ohio Country.

Most of the fighting in the conflict later called the French and Indian War took place back east, largely in the colony of New York and along the St. Lawrence River in New France, but the Ohio River frontier also experienced bloodshed. In July 1755, a force of 2,500 British regular troops and Virginia militiamen (including George Washington) were led into the wilderness of western Pennsylvania by British general Edward Braddock. Braddock's goal was to capture the French Fort Duquesne, near the headwaters of the Ohio River. During the march, Braddock's men were surprised by hundreds of French and their Indian allies, resulting in a massacre of hundreds of British troops. (Not only Washington was present at this frontier battle; Daniel Boone and John Finley were also present, both men serving as wagon teamsters.)

The French and Indian War dragged on until 1763, resulting in victory for the British. The war resulted in tremendous losses for the French in the New World, including territory in New

In the eighteenth century, war broke out between England and France over control of the Ohio Country and other land in North America. Though the British won the French and Indian War after seven years, both sides sufferered significant losses. In this painting, British general William Braddock is ambushed by Native Americans during his attempt to capture Fort Duquesne in Pennsylvania.

France (Canada) and the Ohio Country. Former French forts were occupied by the British, and French frontier settlements along the Ohio River came under the control of the British. With the French removed from the region, colonists moved west in even greater numbers. However, because the presence of increased numbers of trans-Appalachian settlers often upset the Indians living in the vast Ohio Country, the British government passed a law called the Proclamation of 1763, which made it illegal for English colonists to travel across the mountains. This act stated that all the land between the Appalachians and the Mississippi River was for the Indians. Some explorers, such as

Daniel Boone, ignored the law and went west to open up such wilderness areas as Kentucky and Tennessee.

Within a few years of the end of the French and Indian War, the British found themselves fighting a new enemy in the Americas: their own American colonists. The Revolutionary War began in 1775 and lasted until 1783, when the colonists officially gained their independence from the Mother Country. Although most of the fighting of the American Revolution took place east of the Appalachians, at sites such as Brandywine, Pennsylvania; Monmouth Courthouse, New Jersey; and Camden, South Carolina, some of the bloodiest engagements were fought on the frontier in the Ohio Country. Much of this action took place under the direction of a tough-as-nails American frontier fighter, a strapping rifleman in his mid-20s named George Rogers Clark. His plan was to gather a force of frontiersmen, recruits from Ohio and northern Kentucky, march them down the Ohio River, and capture the British outposts in the Illinois Country. These sites were strategic and established centers of frontier populations.

In 1777, after receiving permission from Patrick Henry, then the governor of Virginia, Clark set out across the Appalachian Mountains to seize key British positions in the Ohio Country. He and his men marched and floated along the Ohio River route until they reached the British post at Kaskaskia, a former French settlement established 60 years earlier. Clark and his rangers were able to capture the underdefended southern Illinois outpost without firing a shot. Because most of the remote village's citizens were French, they were surprised to learn that the British and Americans were at war and that France had recently joined in an alliance with the Americans. From there, Clark and his men moved on to the Illinois settlement of Cahokia, where the great Mound Culture had once thrived along the eastern banks of the Mississippi. He then marched to Vincennes, another former French outpost, and its garrison post, Fort Sackville.

Clark's campaigns in Illinois drew the attention of the British commander of Fort Detroit, Lieutenant Colonel Henry Hamilton, who mounted an expedition of hundreds of British troops and Indian allies to rout out Clark from the region of the Mississippi and Ohio Rivers. (Hamilton was notorious on the American frontier for buying scalps from Indians, a practice that earned him the nickname "the Hair Buyer.") Hamilton managed to retake Vincennes and Fort Sackville, because Clark and most of his men had moved on to capture other frontier settlements.

When Clark received word the British had taken back Fort Sackville, he and his men returned to Vincennes, making a legendary winter march through icy waters, facing freezing temperatures. On one occasion, Clark painted his face with war paint and jumped into an icy river to encourage his men to continue their difficult march. In late February 1779, Clark and the Virginia Rangers reached Vincennes and launched a night attack against Hamilton's garrison inside Fort Sackville. Clark later wrote of the engagement:

> Reconnoitered about to find a place to throw up an entrenchment. Found one, and set Capt. Bowman's company to work. Soon crossed the main street, about one hundred and twenty yards from the first gate. . . . The cannon played smartly. Not one of our men wounded. Men in the Fort badly wounded. Fine sport for the sons of Liberty.[16]

During the engagement, rifle and cannon fire lit up the night sky, and the dawn brought surrender from Hamilton.

Clark's campaign across the Ohio River Valley helped loosen British dominance along the frontier and win the Revolutionary War. Clark's military exploits helped secure the region for the United States, and he had an additional impact on the history of the Ohio River. Clark later founded one of the most important of the Ohio's river towns—Louisville, Kentucky—as well as the towns that later became known as Clarksville and New Albany, Indiana.

The American Revolution brought extraordinary change to the 13 colonies engaged in war against the British. Under the agreement ending the war, the Treaty of Paris (1783), the new United States was ceded land from the Atlantic Ocean to the Mississippi River and from the Great Lakes to Spanish Florida. Gone were the British officials, along with the Proclamation of 1763, which had officially closed the frontier to colonial migration. Now it was to be the United States government that would determine future policies regarding the western frontier, including the Ohio River Country. In relatively short order, the Articles of Confederation Congress passed a pair of laws related to the West, especially the Northwest Territory.

By definition, the western border of the United States at the end of the American Revolution was the Mississippi River. The region of the Northwest included the modern-day states of Ohio, Indiana, Illinois, Michigan, and Wisconsin. How government would be organized in those western territories was given extensive attention by Congress. It was determined in 1784 that the western lands would be divided into states and that a western population would first experience territorial status and then statehood. In 1785, the U.S. Congress passed the Land Ordinance of 1785. This congressional act established the machinery for a federally sponsored survey of the Old Northwest and for the sale of western lands.

Congress called for the ordered dividing of the land into square townships, each measuring six miles by six miles. Each township was divided into 36 sections measuring one mile square. There were 640 acres in each section. The land within each section of a township was to then be offered for sale to the public at a price equivalent to $1 per acre. Thus a pioneer immigrant could buy 640 acres, a square mile of territory, for an equal number of dollars. (The amount was equivalent to about $120 in 1990 dollars.)

The original survey in the Old Northwest began in Ohio, along the banks of the Ohio River, at a point where the Ohio River, the eastern border of Ohio, northern Virginia, and western Pennsylvania coincide. From that point, surveyors laid down a geographer's base line to the Muskingum River. The first seven townships extending east-to-west were referred to as the Seven Ranges. This pattern of squares soon became the settlement pattern across the United States, continuing into the Far West and the Great Plains for the next century.

Another act passed by the Articles of Confederation Congress was the Northwest Ordinance of 1787. Under this act, Congress established a governmental system for the Old Northwest. The act allowed for the eventual creation of not more then five and no fewer than three states to be carved out of the region. It also recognized the rights of Americans living there, making them identical to all rights enjoyed by citizens in the original 13 states. Such laws helped organize and streamline western occupation of the territory north of the Ohio River.

White immigration into the Old Northwest became a constant stream of pioneers headed west during the 1780s. In 1787, a Revolutionary War veteran, General Rufus Putnam, led a group of 48 hearty pioneer men downriver from Pittsburgh in a "flatboat, a barge, and three dugout canoes"[17] until they reached the mouth of the Muskingum River. Here they established the first American city in modern-day Ohio, which they named Marietta, after the queen of France, Marie Antoinette, in honor of France's support of the American Revolution. The party of American settlers then went ashore and began building a defense structure, Fort Martius. (Today, a museum in Marietta houses General Putnam's cabin.) Before the year's end, 50 flatboats of frontier families set a course down the Ohio River from Pittsburgh to occupy new lands.

The following year, nearly 5,000 emigrants reached Fort Harmar during the first six months alone. A significant number of those who migrated into the Ohio Valley to occupy land claims were veterans of the Revolutionary War who had received land from the Congress to compensate them for their service to their new country. Many of these new residents of the Ohio Country were New Englanders, but they came from many eastern locales. A Connecticut man named Moses Cleaveland brought 50 pioneers into Ohio to occupy the tract known as the

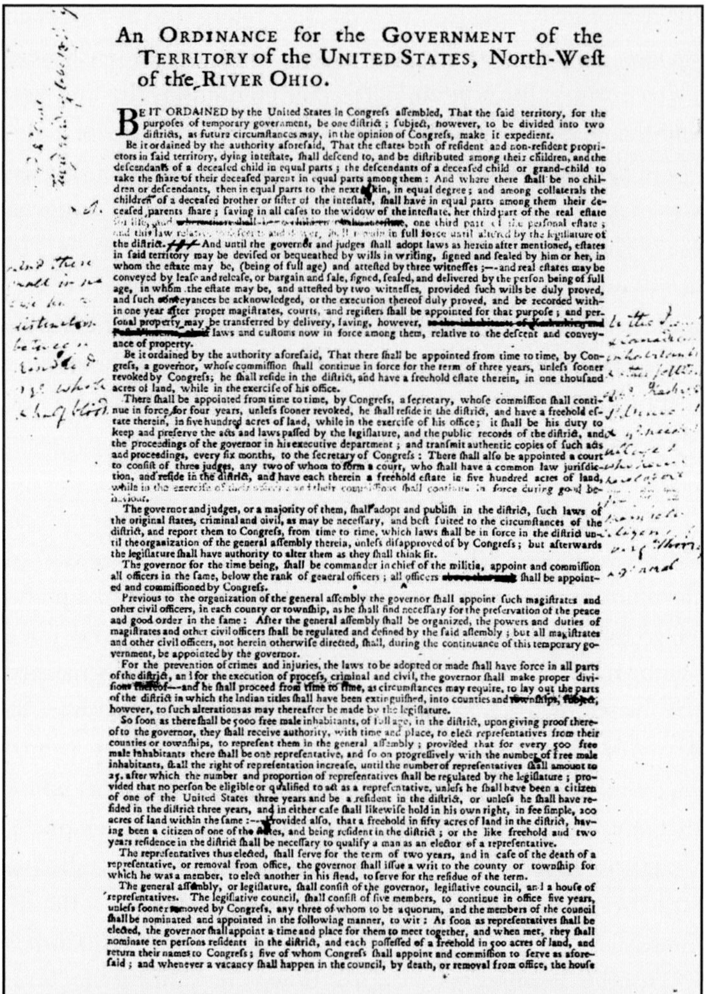

An ORDINANCE for the GOVERNMENT of the TERRITORY of the UNITED STATES, North-Weſt of the RIVER OHIO.

BE IT ORDAINED by the United States in Congreſs aſſembled, That the ſaid territory, for the purpoſes of temporary government, be one diſtrict; ſubject, however, to be divided into two diſtricts, as future circumſtances may, in the opinion of Congreſs, make it expedient.

Be it ordained by the authority aforeſaid, That the eſtates both of reſident and non-reſident proprietors in ſaid territory, dying inteſtate, ſhall deſcend to, and be diſtributed among their children, and the deſcendants of a deceaſed child in equal parts; the deſcendants of a deceaſed child or grand-child to take the ſhare of their deceaſed parent in equal parts among them: And where there ſhall be no children or deſcendants, then in equal parts to the next of kin, in equal degree; and among collaterals the children of a deceaſed brother or ſiſter of the inteſtate, ſhall have in equal parts among them their deceaſed parents ſhare; ſaving in all caſes to the widow of the inteſtate, her third part of the real eſtate for life, and [illegible], one third part of the perſonal eſtate; and this law relative to deſcent and dower, ſhall remain in full force until altered by the legiſlature of the diſtrict. And until the governor and judges ſhall adopt laws as herein after mentioned, eſtates in ſaid territory may be deviſed or bequeathed by wills in writing, ſigned and ſealed by him or her, in whom the eſtate may be, (being of full age) and atteſted by three witneſſes;—and real eſtates may be conveyed by leaſe and releaſe, or bargain and ſale, ſigned, ſealed, and delivered by the perſon being of full age, in whom the eſtate may be, and atteſted by two witneſſes, provided ſuch wills be duly proved, and ſuch conveyances be acknowledged, or the execution thereof duly proved, and be recorded within one year after proper magiſtrates, courts, and regiſters ſhall be appointed for that purpoſe; and perſonal property may be transferred by delivery, ſaving, however, [illegible] laws and cuſtoms now in force among them, relative to the deſcent and conveyance of property.

Be it ordained by the authority aforeſaid, That there ſhall be appointed from time to time, by Congreſs, a governor, whoſe commiſſion ſhall continue in force for the term of three years, unleſs ſooner revoked by Congreſs; he ſhall reſide in the diſtrict, and have a freehold eſtate therein, in one thouſand acres of land, while in the exerciſe of his office.

There ſhall be appointed from time to time, by Congreſs, a ſecretary, whoſe commiſſion ſhall continue in force for four years, unleſs ſooner revoked, he ſhall reſide in the diſtrict, and have a freehold eſtate therein, in five hundred acres of land, while in the exerciſe of his office; it ſhall be his duty to keep and preſerve the acts and laws paſſed by the legiſlature, and the public records of the diſtrict, and the proceedings of the governor in his executive department; and tranſmit authentic copies of ſuch acts and proceedings, every ſix months, to the ſecretary of Congreſs: There ſhall alſo be appointed a court to conſiſt of three judges, any two of whom to form a court, who ſhall have a common law juriſdiction, and reſide in the diſtrict, and have each therein a freehold eſtate in five hundred acres of land, while in the exerciſe of their offices; and their commiſſions ſhall continue in force during good behaviour.

The governor and judges, or a majority of them, ſhall adopt and publiſh in the diſtrict, ſuch laws of the original ſtates, criminal and civil, as may be neceſſary, and beſt ſuited to the circumſtances of the diſtrict, and report them to Congreſs, from time to time, which laws ſhall be in force in the diſtrict until the organization of the general aſſembly therein, unleſs diſapproved of by Congreſs; but afterwards the legiſlature ſhall have authority to alter them as they ſhall think fit.

The governor for the time being, ſhall be commander in chief of the militia, appoint and commiſſion all officers in the ſame, below the rank of general officers; all officers [illegible] ſhall be appointed and commiſſioned by Congreſs.

Previous to the organization of the general aſſembly the governor ſhall appoint ſuch magiſtrates and other civil officers, in each county or townſhip, as he ſhall find neceſſary for the preſervation of the peace and good order in the ſame: After the general aſſembly ſhall be organized, the powers and duties of magiſtrates and other civil officers ſhall be regulated and defined by the ſaid aſſembly; but all magiſtrates and other civil officers, not herein otherwiſe directed, ſhall, during the continuance of this temporary government, be appointed by the governor.

For the prevention of crimes and injuries, the laws to be adopted or made ſhall have force in all parts of the diſtrict, and for the execution of proceſs, criminal and civil, the governor ſhall make proper diviſions thereof—and he ſhall proceed from time to time, as circumſtances may require, to lay out the parts of the diſtrict in which the Indian titles ſhall have been extinguiſhed, into counties and townſhips, ſubject, however, to ſuch alterations as may thereafter be made by the legiſlature.

So ſoon as there ſhall be 5000 free male inhabitants, of full age, in the diſtrict, upon giving proof thereof to the governor, they ſhall receive authority, with time and place, to elect repreſentatives from their counties or townſhips, to repreſent them in the general aſſembly; provided that for every 500 free male inhabitants there ſhall be one repreſentative, and ſo on progreſſively with the number of free male inhabitants, ſhall the right of repreſentation increaſe, until the number of repreſentatives ſhall amount to 25, after which the number and proportion of repreſentatives ſhall be regulated by the legiſlature; provided that no perſon be eligible or qualified to act as a repreſentative, unleſs he ſhall have been a citizen of one of the United States three years and be a reſident in the diſtrict, or unleſs he ſhall have reſided in the diſtrict three years, and in either caſe ſhall likewiſe hold in his own right, in fee ſimple, 200 acres of land within the ſame:—provided alſo, that a freehold in fifty acres of land in the diſtrict, having been a citizen of one of the ſtates, and being reſident in the diſtrict; or the like freehold and two years reſidence in the diſtrict ſhall be neceſſary to qualify a man as an elector of a repreſentative.

The repreſentatives thus elected, ſhall ſerve for the term of two years, and in caſe of the death of a repreſentative, or removal from office, the governor ſhall iſſue a writ to the county or townſhip for which he was a member, to elect another in his ſtead, to ſerve for the reſidue of the term.

The general aſſembly, or legiſlature, ſhall conſiſt of the governor, legiſlative council, and a houſe of repreſentatives. The legiſlative council, ſhall conſiſt of five members, to continue in office five years, unleſs ſooner removed by Congreſs, any three of whom to be a quorum, and the members of the council ſhall be nominated and appointed in the following manner, to wit: As ſoon as repreſentatives ſhall be elected, the governor ſhall appoint a time and place for them to meet together, and when met, they ſhall nominate ten perſons reſidents in the diſtrict, and each poſſeſſed of a freehold in 500 acres of land, and return their names to Congreſs; five of whom Congreſs ſhall appoint and commiſſion to ſerve as aforeſaid; and whenever a vacancy ſhall happen in the council, by death, or removal from office, the houſe

Following the American Revolution, the United States government had to develop new policies regarding the western frontier. One act was the Northwest Ordinance of 1787, which allowed for the creation of several new states west of the Ohio River and recognized the rights of Americans already living in the territory.

Western Reserve, lands "bordering on Lake Erie which Connecticut had not ceded to the Federal Government."[18] The Seven Ranges, Ohio lands lying just south of the Western

Reserve, drew immigrants from Pennsylvania. To the west, the Scioto Valley drew new residents from Virginia, who established Chillicothe as their primary frontier community. Farther west, the Ohio lured Kentuckians north. The region soon became a melting pot of ethnic and national groups, including English, Irish, Scots, Germans, and others. The movement continued for decades. As Morris Birkbeck, as English traveler described the movement into the Old Northwest after walking the National Road across western Pennsylvania, "Old America seems to be breaking up and moving westward. We are seldom out of sight, as we travel on this grand track, towards the Ohio, of family groups, behind and before us."[19]

Although such frontier-related acts as the Land Ordinance of 1785 and the Northwest Ordinance of 1787 were among the few successful pieces of legislation passed under the Articles of Confederation government, the western migration they inspired created problems for Native Americans in the region. The handwriting was already on the wall for the tribes of the northern Ohio Country. Under two additional Indian treaties, the second Treaty of Fort Stanwix (1784) and the Treaty of Fort McIntosh (1785), the Iroquois and several Ohio tribes were forced to surrender ownership of part of their traditional lands in eastern Ohio. This was all done hastily and under duress, pushing the Indians out of the way so that the region could be surveyed and parceled out to willing frontiersmen.

Desperate for a national cash flow, Congress quickly sold 1.5 million acres of this land. In fact, land sales outstripped the survey, and thousands of western migrants poured into Ohio and occupied land without a clear title or purchase. In 1785, Congress ordered national troops into Ohio to remove the interlopers, but the squatters returned after the soldiers left. Despite its results, the Northwest Ordinance of 1787 did attempt to redraw relations between the U.S. government and the Ohio Country Indians. Under the act, Congress recognized the independence of the Indian nations, but the government continued to use military force against tribes who were unwilling to cede land to the whites. Thus, a cycle of Indian land cessions continued. A raging bitterness continued to develop among Ohio tribes, and they finally took military action of their own. In 1790, such tribes as the Shawnees, Delawares, and others united under Chief Little Turtle.

That fall, Little Turtle and his warriors fought a contingent of troops under the command of General Josiah Harmar in Ohio and defeated them badly. A year later, in November 1791, the same Indians crushed forces led by General Arthur St. Clair, the governor of the Northwest Territory, killing or wounding nearly 1,000 men. The loss would stand as the worst defeat inflicted by Indians on an army in American history. Such successes prompted the British in Canada to ally themselves in spirit with the Ohio Indians. The British built a new post, Fort Miami, in northern Ohio and met with Indians there.

St. Clair's defeat prompted President George Washington to dispatch a significant force of American troops into the Ohio frontier under the command of General Anthony Wayne. Known as "Mad Anthony," Wayne engaged the Indians in the Battle of Fallen Timbers on August 20, 1794. The northern Ohio battle was a crushing blow to the Indians. When the defeated warriors attempted to take sanctuary among the British at Fort Miami, they found the gate of the frontier fortress closed to them. "Mad" Anthony Wayne's victory at Fallen Timbers in the fall of 1794 was a destructive blow to the Ohio Country tribes. Under such a great loss, the warriors were forced to agree to new land negotiations called the Treaty of Greenville (1795). This treaty called for the Indians to cede the southern half of Ohio and a portion of Indiana to the United States. In addition, the Northwest Territory settlements of towns such as Detroit, as well as the newer, small settlement of Chicago, on Lake Michigan, were also granted to American control.

This treaty gave the American government a new footing in the frontier region. It solidified its strength and furthered its legitimacy in the West as a true nation with regional power. It also opened the way for additional American migration into and settlement of the Ohio River Valley.

The Ohio remained one of the most important natural resources available to the white pioneers of the Old Northwest, as well as Kentucky and Tennessee. Trans-Appalachian pioneer farmers, producing everything from corn, hemp, and wheat to hogs, cotton, and whiskey, needed access to viable markets for their agricultural produce. Hauling their goods overland by freight wagon was especially prohibitive because of the high costs. Instead, thousands of western Americans each year would build flatboats; load them with baskets of corn, bushels of wheat, bales of cotton, jugs of whiskey, or herds of hogs; float their wares down local rivers—the Tennessee, Cumberland, Wabash, and others—to the Ohio River; and then continue down that lengthy trade stream to the Mississippi.

Ultimately, these intrepid pioneer boatman would reach the port of New Orleans, where they could sell their goods, accumulate much needed cash, and then make their way back to their homes in Tennessee, Kentucky, or Ohio on horseback or on foot, traveling overland across a heavily forested trail called the Natchez Trace.

By 1800, the number of pioneers living in the West lying between the Appalachians and the Mississippi had reached 500,000. Many of them had come originally from Virginia and North Carolina in search of inexpensive yet fertile farmland. They settled along the various west-flowing rivers of the region, including the Tennessee, the Cumberland, and, of course, the Ohio. Two states already had been carved out of the backwoods settlements—Kentucky (1792) and Tennessee (1796)—making them the 15th and 16th states in the Union.

This movement of Americans knew no bounds during the years just prior to and just after 1800. Americans were restless, seeing greater opportunities over the next horizon. For that reason, every year nearly 1 out of every 10 American families moved. Throughout the Atlantic Coast states, approximately one in three rural families had moved between the 1790 and 1800 censuses. Many such moves were simply lateral, involving a short

CINCINNATI: FRONTIER URBAN SUCCESS STORY

The increase in land routes into the Ohio Country brought the establishment of more western outposts, villages, and landings on the Ohio River. Despite the rural nature of the western settlements, some communities of significance were established. One of the most important towns on the frontier by 1800 was Cincinnati, Ohio. Situated 450 miles to the west of Pittsburgh, Cincinnati was founded in 1788 as the settlement of Losantville by Mathias Denman. Within two years, Losantville was renamed "Cincinnati" after the highly popular Revolutionary War veterans organization, the Society of the Cincinnati. In its early years, Cincinnati was little more than a fort intended to protect pioneers living along the Ohio and Miami Rivers. Indian attacks were common, and violence involving the Shawnee and Miami Indians caused the region to be known as "the Slaughterhouse." After the 1794 defeat of the Indians in the Battle of Fallen Timbers, Cincinnati was on its way up. The town developed, becoming a popular site of departure for frontier families headed down the Ohio River, bound for Indiana, Illinois, or Kentucky. At the turn of the century, Cincinnati was home to 750 people, but by 1810, nearly 2,500 lived there.

In time, Cincinnati became more than an important river town on the American frontier. It developed as a significant western meat-packing center, with facilities for the slaughter of hogs, causing frontier citizens to refer to the town as "Porkopolis." Other industries, including soap, shoe, boot, and candle—all derived from animal by-products—manufacturing, were thriving in the diversified economy of frontier Cincinnati. The growth of such western cities could not be ignored with the passage of each decade of the 1800s. No city west of the Appalachians was among the top 10 in population even as late as 1820 (except for French New Orleans), but by 1850, the top 10 list included Cincinnati, New Orleans, St. Louis, Pittsburgh, and Louisville, Kentucky. Three of those five were Ohio River towns. Today, Cincinnati remains one of the most important cities on the Ohio River, and its long, productive history continues to earn this significant river city the title of "Queen City of the West."

distance between rural communities or towns. Many others moved greater distances, totaling hundreds of miles. To facilitate these migrations, the western settlers used the various rivers of the region to float their families, household items, and livestock by flatboat to greener pastures.

As more and more Americans eyed this rich region, the young United States government helped develop the routes into Ohio. In 1796, President George Washington was authorized by Congress to contract with Ebenezer Zane to establish a trail across Ohio. Zane, a resident of Maryland, began to carve his trail at Wheeling, Virginia (now in the state of West Virginia) and into southeast Ohio. The route crossed into the eastern portion of the territory to a site located along the banks of the Muskingum River. There, Zane established a community he called Zanesville. He opened a ferry there to bring settlers across the Muskingum River. In time, Zane extended his trail to the Ohio and Kentucky Rivers to a settlement called Limestone. Zane's Trace was one of the first non-Indian trails in Ohio, and it would later serve as a portion of a major highway across the frontier, the National Road.

With great enthusiasm and high hopes for better lives, thousands of Americans moved into the Ohio Country. They crossed over difficult mountain trails, walked along primitive roads, and navigated unsteady western rivers in search of a new place and a new identity as the first of those to settle the great expanse of American land that stretched from the low-lying Appalachians to the broad expanses of the distant Mississippi River, which lay mysteriously 1,000 miles to the west.

4

"A Prospect of Commerce"

Even before the Revolutionary War, British subjects began moving west across the Appalachian Mountains into the western lands of modern-day Kentucky, Tennessee, Ohio, and Indiana. The growth of the American population during the period from 1790 to 1800 nearly demanded that the new republic look to the west for expansion. Within that decade, the number of Americans increased from 3.9 million to 5.3 million. The frontier deterrent represented by Indians was also largely eliminated by 1795, with the signing of the Treaty of Greenville, which called for the Indians to surrender the southern half of Ohio plus a small portion of Indiana. That same year, an American diplomat, Thomas Pinckney, negotiated a treaty with the Spanish to open up the Mississippi River for river traffic and trade. The Spanish had completely closed New Orleans to American river trade between 1784 and 1788. Since 1788, the Spanish had allowed Americans to sell their produce in New Orleans only after they paid customs duties. The new agreement gave Americans the "right of deposit," allowing them to offload their flatboats and river barges and store their produce, without paying a duty, until an American ship arrived to carry the frontier produce to markets overseas.

The Pinckney Treaty was greeted with great enthusiasm across the trans-Appalachian frontier. The Americans on the frontier needed access to the Mississippi River and the Spanish-controlled port of New Orleans for shipping their frontier produce to market. Both of these treaties pointed the Americans not only to the west but also down the Ohio River toward the Mississippi.

This period of American history, from the 1780s through the great Mississippi steamboat years before the Civil War, saw many different kinds of rivercraft used on the western rivers. Among the earliest and most important types were flatboats and keelboats. These two types of boats carried much of the farm produce raised by Ohio Valley farmers. The first flatboats could be found on the Ohio River. Such a boat was built for rivers, because its flat bottom allowed it to float safely in as little as a few feet of water. A flatboat was not really a boat but rather a big, floating box, which almost anyone with the right tools could build. It had a rectangular shape, and its sides stood about five feet high. Flatboats came in different sizes, according to their purposes, ranging in length from 20 to 100 feet and 10 to 25 feet in width. The average flatboat was 12 to 14 feet wide and nearly 50 feet long.

Life on a flatboat moved at a slow pace. The average flatboat needed a five-person crew to work the sweeps and do the cooking, which was often done on deck on a fire built over a sandbox. Floating down the Ohio and Mississippi Rivers from Pittsburgh to New Orleans was nearly a 2,000 mile trip, the voyage taking between five and six weeks with the boat traveling 24 hours a day. In time, the world of rivermen became one of rowdy labor and transient social structures. Historian Richard Bartlett describes life among the western American flatboat men:

> There were professional flatboatmen who spent their lives on the western waters. They were tough, arrogant, and illiterate; they loved to exchange boasts, insults, threats dares, and profanity with people along the shore, and in time every river town had its gambling dens, saloons, and brothels to cater to them. The boatmen often supplied free transportation, liquor, and food to one of the itinerant fiddlers who plied the river offering in exchange for the hospitality a storehouse of songs—love songs, jigs, profane ditties, but few sacred numbers—as well as river gossip. Sometimes the men all danced on the deck, or gambled, or fought.[20]

During the early decades of the 1800s, between 400 and 700 flatboats arrived in New Orleans every year. The year 1847 was the busiest for flatboats: More than 2,600 flatboats made the trip from the Ohio River to New Orleans. Certainly, hundreds more landed at ports farther upriver.

Another western rivercraft was the keelboat. This boat was very different from a flatboat, because it was a permanent craft. It was much more expensive to build than a flatboat, costing between $2,000 and $3,000. Keelboats had "professional" crews that carried western goods downriver for a fee. Typically, a

Many different types of rivercraft were popular in America from the late eighteenth century through the Civil War. One of the earliest types was the flatboat, such as the one in this painting carrying pioneers down the Ohio River. The flatboat's smooth bottom allowed it to float in just a few feet of water, but it moved very slowly, taking almost six weeks to make a 2,000-mile trip from Pittsburgh to New Orleans.

keelboat could deliver a ton of cargo upriver cheaper than the cargo could be carried overland by wagon.

A keelboat was built with a four-square-inch strip of timber called a keel running from bow to stern. The boats were generally 60 to 70 feet long and featured a cargo hold three or four feet deep. The boats were pointed at both the bow and the stern. A box-shaped cabin covered the center of the deck. Keelboats usually had a center mast with a sail, and most required a crew of about 10.

On each side of the keelboat's deck was a walkway where the crew could "pole" the boat upriver. To do this, each person would take a turn pushing a long pole into the river bottom and "walking" the boat upstream. These setting poles were usually about 12 to 14 feet long and capped with iron. Cleats were nailed across the walkway to give the polers something to push against as they walked. If the river current was too strong, the crew was forced to cordelle the boat. In this method, the crew used long ropes tied to a tree onshore and pulled the boat upstream.

Working as a professional keelboater was a hard job. Like flatboat men, keelboaters were often rough and tough. The pay was adequate for the time but not extravagant. In the early 1800s, the captain of a keelboat was paid $100 for a three-month stint on the river. His deckhands received between $20 and $50.

Perhaps the most legendary keelboater was Mike Fink. Born near Pittsburgh in 1780, Fink served as a scout in the Indian wars of the 1790s. Later, he owned and operated two keelboats. Fink was a great bragger who would challenge anyone to a variety of contests. His famous boasting was often an unlikely combination of superlatives and frontier arrogance: "I can hit like fourth-proof lightnin' an' every lick I make in the woods lets in an acre o' sunshine. I can out-run, out-jump, out-shoot, out-brag, out-drink, an' out-fight—rough-an'-tumble; no holts barred—ary man on both sides the river from Pittsburgh to New Orleans an' back ag'in to St. Louie."[21] Fink's river career lasted from 1790 to 1822. In 1822, he was shot by a companion during a fur-trading expedition on the Missouri River.

No matter how one floated, steered, or poled the Ohio River in the early 1800s, travel on the river could be dangerous, not just because of the unstable and raw condition of the river itself but also because of robbers and river pirates. On the Lower Ohio, less than 100 miles from Cairo, Illinois, there was no place more notorious than Cave-in-Rock, a "high, flat-faced cliff jutting up on the Illinois shore, with a huge, dark hole more than twenty feet high near the bottom."[22] This peculiar rock formation became a favorite of river pirates who worked in gangs and terrorized many families and flatboat men who entered their portion of the river. Such river riffraff often paddled out to a flatboat or keelboat, subdued and killed the crew, and then took possession of the boat's cargo, running it downriver and selling it for a profit. It was only after the seizure of many boat cargoes that a group of Pittsburgh merchants hired a small army of recruits and sent them down the Ohio to clear out the river pirates.

Everyone from Indians to the white pioneers of the early 1800s moved along the Ohio River with a wide variety of river craft from canoes to flatboats to keelboats, but all these methods of river travel lacked one important capacity: They were great for floating down the Ohio River but were either difficult or impossible to deliver back upstream. By the early 1800s, that particular river travel problem was about to be solved with the invention of the steamboat.

The first successful steamboats in America were built back east, along the Hudson River, plying their courses up and down the river from Albany, the capital of New York, to New York City, one of the great East Coast harbors of the era. This new form of river craft soon found its way to the Mississippi River.

One of the greatest American inventors, Robert Fulton, built and launched his *Clermont* in 1807, less than a year after Lewis and Clark returned from their western explorations. In just a few short years, the steamboat proved to be practical, innovative, and commercially viable. As Americans were pouring west by the thousands, it did not take long before Fulton was ready to take his transportation innovation to the West. Fulton joined in this venture with two partners: Robert Livingston, a well-known New York political figure (he had signed the Declaration of Independence back in 1776) and entrepreneur, and Nicholas J. Roosevelt. (Two of Roosevelt's descendents, Theodore and Franklin, later became U.S. presidents.)

Roosevelt's construction of the first western river steamboat began in 1810. Nicholas J. Roosevelt laid the keel for his boat in the summer of 1810 near the frontier town of Pittsburgh, at the headwaters of the Ohio River, where the Monongahela and the Allegheny Rivers join together to form the great western flowing artery that flows into the Mississippi River. The boat was launched a year later, in March 1811. When Roosevelt finished his boat, it was a side-wheeler, meaning that the paddle wheel that propelled the boat along the river was built on the side of the boat. Roosevelt's wife christened their paddle-wheel steamboat *New Orleans*. Critics of Roosevelt's boat called it a "dainty teakettle," and predicted that the boat would be no match for the rough river ahead and the equally tough men who made their living—both legally and illegally—along the river.[23]

On September 10, 1811, the Roosevelts began their trip down the Ohio, bound for the Mississippi and New Orleans, with a small crew and the family dog, a Newfoundland named Tiger. Roosevelt had high hopes that his boat would make the 2,000-mile trip successfully and prove to others that the western rivers could be tapped for steamboat service as eastern rivers were. As they made their way down river, the Roosevelts stopped at each Ohio River town. When they reached the Kentucky town of Louisville, Mrs. Roosevelt gave birth to a son onboard the *New Orleans.*

In December, the *New Orleans* reached the Mississippi River. Under normal conditions, the trip down the two great American rivers might have been a peaceful one. The Roosevelts, however, faced serious challenges, including finding themselves in the midst of one of the most severe earthquakes in the history of North America. The December 6 earthquake was centered along the Mississippi River near the Missouri Bootheel community of New Madrid. The earthquake caused the earth to ripple and, at one point, the Mississippi River actually flowed backward. The quake was so severe it caused churchbells to ring in Richmond, Virginia, and plaster walls to crack in Baltimore. The quake also created a maze of debris and floating trees, making it difficult for the *New Orleans* to continue its trip downriver. In his book *The Mississippi and the Making of a Nation*, historian Stephen Ambrose describes these obstacles:

> Entire towns along the Mississippi were destroyed. Islands crumbled into the river, limestone cliffs tumbled into the debris-filled water, and recurrent tremors jangled everyone's nerves. . . . The *New Orleans* survived the quake, but the crew's journey suddenly became a harrowing obstacle course. Wherever the boat anchored, the crew had to cut through trees that had been felled by the quake and lay blocking the channel. Treacherous new snags and sandbars had appeared. Only with great difficulty did

A SAD CENTENNIAL VOYAGE

One hundred years after the introduction of the first steamboat on the Ohio River—the *New Orleans,* built by Nicholas Roosevelt—the river was experiencing one of its most depressing eras.

There was little commercial traffic on the river during the early twentieth century. Yet several entrepreneurs were determined to remind Americans of the centennial of the original western steamer. A reconstruction of the *New Orleans* was built in Pittsburgh (just as the original steamer had been) and launched on the Ohio in November 1911. Amid local fanfare, the newly launched steamboat fired its signal cannon and "began an anniversary voyage down the Ohio and the Mississippi."[*]

The timing of the launch and maiden voyage of the second *New Orleans* could not have been at a worse time on the Ohio. In the words of one area reporter, "Never before has Ohio river tonnage been so worthless."[**] As the commemorative vessel plied its way down river, it was plagued by dreary weather and recurring downpours, her "pennants dripping with November rain."[***] The river was nearly lifeless, and the *New Orleans* passed dozens of river communities, their moorings empty, with only "shantyboats in the bare willows, and an occasional coal tow creeping around a bend."[+] River celebrations were sparse as the *New Orleans* continued down the Ohio to the Mississippi until finally reaching its destination at the port of New Orleans. Having generated little interest, the owners of the *New Orleans* steamer chose to make no return upriver and put the steamboat up for sale, a sad end to a well-intended tribute to the first trans-Appalachian steamer.

* Quoted in Walter Havighurst, *River to the West,* 257.
** Ibid.
*** Ibid.
\+ Ibid.

> the crew find passage between rocky islands, sandbars, and driftwood scattered in bewildering new patterns.[24]

The New Madrid Earthquake soon became a series of quakes epicentered along the middle Mississippi River, and the *New Orleans* experienced them all. The crew onboard watched as the West's first steamboat passed river towns, all abandoned, left desolate and destroyed in the aftermath of the quakes. While on the river, life was frightening enough, as the river became a waterway crowded with dangerous debris. Those onboard also experienced an additional fear as they tied up at the river's banks, where "their most dreaded task was cutting down trees for fuel each night when the earth trembled beneath their feet. . ."[25]

As Indians watched the *New Orleans* paddle past their river settlements on the Mississippi, they were frightened by the smoke-belching, noisy craft. The Chickasaws called the boat a "fire canoe." Some even blamed the *New Orleans* for creating the earthquake as its paddle wheels stirred up the river water. For much of the nineteenth century, many Indians remained skeptical of the steamboat and refused to take passage on the boats they called "European devils."[26]

Despite the challenges the Roosevelts and their crew faced on the Mississippi, the underpowered *New Orleans* managed to make it down river and arrive at its Louisiana port city namesake on January 12, 1812. The boat's arrival in New Orleans heralded a serious change in the future of the Mississippi River. As Roosevelt's steamboat passed Natchez, Mississippi, one elderly black man, the slave of a planter named Samuel Davis, standing along the river's banks watched as the boat chugged by and commented, "Ole Mississippi done met her master now!"[27]

After the successful 1811–12 voyage of the *New Orleans* down two of America's great inland rivers, Fulton and Livingston organized a steamboat enterprise on the Ohio, known as the Ohio Steamboat Navigation Company. (The company was actually chartered in Indiana in 1810, before Roosevelt's *New Orleans* was even completed.) Investors could purchase stock in the company with an investment of $50,000. The company soon constructed two additional steamboats—the *Vesuvius* and the *Aetna,* both named for volcanoes in Italy and Sicily, both unfortunate references, because early steamboats gained a reputation for exploding. With his three riverboats, Fulton intended to cover the entire distance from New Orleans to Pittsburgh. The *New Orleans* would run up the Mississippi to Natchez; *Vesuvius* would cover the rivers between Natchez and Louisville, Kentucky; and the *Aetna* would deliver cargo and passengers from Louisville to Pittsburgh.

Fulton's intent was to gain a monopoly on steamboating on the Ohio between Pittsburgh and New Orleans, just as he had been granted sole steamboat rights on the Hudson River back east. However, others jumped into the game quickly. A western boatman named Henry M. Shreve built a steamboat with a flat bottom and a high pressure steam engine, allowing him to pilot his newly designed rivercraft up the Mississippi and Ohio, a feat Roosevelt's *New Orleans* had been unable to accomplish. Shreve's inspiration for a new steamboat design was a boat built in Pittsburgh by Daniel French, the *Comet*. French's boat was fitted with a high-pressure, noncondensing engine, and it did complete one trip from Pittsburgh to New Orleans before suffering mechanical failure on its return trip. Their mutual interest drove Shreve and French to go into business together, establishing the Monongahela and Ohio Steamboat Company in Brownsville, Pennsylvania, in 1813, as a direct challenge to Fulton.

Shreve and French collaborated in the building of a steamboat they called *Enterprise*, completed in 1814. It was fitted with a paddle wheel at its stern, was 80 feet long, and had a cargo capacity of 75 tons. The *Enterprise* was launched on December 1, 1814, just at the end of the War of 1812. In fact, the boat's first cargo consisted of guns and ammunition for General Andrew Jackson's army, then encamped near the mouth of the Mississippi River. The *Enterprise*'s engine allowed her to make the trip from Pittsburgh to New Orleans in just two weeks! After delivering the needed ordnance, the *Enterprise* spent several weeks moving supplies and troops around and near the city of New Orleans, taking fire from British guns on one occasion. After the Battle of New Orleans in early January 1815, the *Enterprise* left the city and returned upriver to Louisville by May and then to Pittsburgh the following month.

The success of the *Enterprise* did not go unnoticed. One Pennsylvania newspaper wrote excitedly, "[The *Enterprise*] is the first steamboat that ever made the voyage to the mouth of the Mississippi and back. . . . She was only thirty-four days in actual service in making her voyage, which our readers will remember must be performed against power currents, and is upwards of 2,200 miles in length."[28] Another paper clearly saw the future in steamboating, as the *Niles' Weekly Register*, published in Baltimore, exulted, "How do the rivers and canals of the old world dwindle into insignificance compared with this, and what a prospect of commerce is held out to the immense regions of the West by the means of these boats."[29]

Shreve did not bask in the success of his *Enterprise* but instead built another Ohio–Mississippi River steamer, the *Washington*. His newer model featured such innovations as the placement of the engines on the main deck rather than below. The engines were more powerful, and there was more room for freight—the capacity reaching 400 tons—but the *Washington* gained notoriety as the first western riverboat to explode. During her maiden voyage on the Ohio in the summer of 1816, as the *Washington* passed the river town of Marietta, Ohio, one of the boilers blew up, killing 10 onboard and injuring several, including Shreve himself. After completing repairs over the following months, Shreve put the *Washington* back in service.

Three years after Shreve and French established their Ohio River company, another line, the Gallatin–Ohio Steamboat Company, received a charter from the state of Kentucky to operate on the Ohio River. These early companies did not establish regular service on the river; instead, they arrived at river towns with a haphazard, hit-or-miss approach caused by the unreliability of their boats. A succession of river steamers followed by the 1820s and 1830s, each making its individual contribution to the history of the nineteenth century and the development, progress, and settlement of the Ohio River Valley.

As hundreds of thousands of Americans migrated into the trans-Appalachian region, they established hundreds of frontier outposts. Many of these early settlements would remain small, unlikely places for western development. A handful of others were destined to become important river towns and cities. In each settlement, whether large or small, those who established their homes in the region created economies "whose general outlines would not change substantially until the coming of the railroad."[30] Much of the effort to create frontier economies along the river took place during the first two decades of the nineteenth century. In 1801, before a single steamboat had reached any western river, the value of all trade goods shipped downriver on the Ohio and other inland rivers to New Orleans was $3.6 million. By 1816, with the help of steam power on America's rivers, that figure had more than doubled to $8 million.

Such increases gave rise to not only such an important Mississippi River port as New Orleans, but to Ohio River towns as well. From its river vantage at the headwaters of the Ohio, Pittsburgh became, from 1800 to 1815, one of the most important and productive towns on the Ohio River. From its origins as a French fort (Fort Duquesne) to its British takeover and renaming as Fort Pitt (after the English prime minister who saw his country to victory during the French and Indian War), the town of Pittsburgh grew faster than many frontier settlements. The town enjoyed the advantage of commanding the trade along three rivers (the Ohio and its sources, the Monongahela and Allegheny). The numbers indicate Pittsburgh's growth. Between 1800 and 1815, the town's population increased five times over (from 1,500 to 8,000). Pittsburgh served as a middleman in the frontier trade, connecting downriver producers, mostly farmers, to markets in Philadelphia, along the primitive roads of the period. It also provided a stop for those migrating west. When such immigrants "arrived at the head of the Ohio, they needed nearly everything—food, furniture, and even clothing."[31] By 1820, Pittsburgh could boast "sixty three shops, including twenty three general stores."[32] The town's commerce also centered on river trade and a developing system of craftsmen, blacksmiths, wheelwrights, and other frontier artisans. Along Pittsburgh's primitive streets, immigrants could find a glass factory, brewery, and a small shipbuilding yard. By 1830, Pittsburgh had established itself as a western iron producer, having its own rolling mill, steam-powered hammering system, and a factory system.

Other river towns developed along the same tracks as Pittsburgh, if on a smaller scale.

5

Days of Steam and War

Regularly scheduled steamboat traffic on the Ohio River became commonplace by the 1830s and 1840s. As early as 1840, in fact, riverboats steaming up and down both the Ohio and Mississippi Rivers had delivered only 3,000 fewer tons of cargo than the entire merchant fleet of the British Empire. (By 1852, the Ohio River town of Cincinnati saw 8,000 steamboats arrive and depart from its wharves, the equivalent of a paddle-wheeler an hour!) As early as 1826, the Cincinnati and Louisville U.S. Mail Line was in business, boating between those two river towns and delivering mail three times a week. Five years later, the line was making departures from each river port on a daily basis. Packet service—a boat that works the river on a regular, published schedule and delivers freight, passengers, and mail—originated in Pittsburgh in 1835, when the Pittsburgh and Louisville Line, with a fleet of a dozen boats, opened operations on the river. A year later, the Good Intent Line and the Ohio Pilot's Line began running to Louisville. An additional line ran from Pittsburgh to St. Louis on the Mississippi. An economic depression beginning in 1837 brought financial disaster to several of these lines, putting them out of business.

By 1842, regular packet service was back, as the Cincinnati and Pittsburgh Packet Line took to the river. The eight boats of the C&PPL carried large numbers of European immigrants into the western frontier of nineteenth-century America. The 1850s brought a significant rival to the packet traffic on the Ohio River: the railroad. As rail lines were laid across the region served by the river steamers, they posed a singular challenge to the riverboats and their monopoly on fast, efficient commerce, as well as passenger service. Some riverboat lines worked out deals with railways to connect their services. The Union Line of steamboats was in operation by 1853, running between Wheeling (in modern-day West Virginia) and Louisville, working in tandem with the Baltimore and Ohio Railroad, whose tracks extended from Baltimore to Wheeling.

Despite such agreements, the railroads eventually spelled doom for the continuation of extensive riverboat traffic on the Ohio River.

The age of the steamboats on the Ohio brought great advances in urbanization and commercial development to the Ohio Valley. Against this backdrop of rapid change on the Ohio River, the region was experiencing another form of change, as the United States appeared set on a course of ultimate dissolution over the issue of the expansion of slavery. Just as the Ohio was a turbulent river, so the times were politically turbulent. In a sense, the Ohio River was at the center of the ever-expanding national split over slavery. It was the Ohio that formed the longest boundary between the slave-holding southern states and the northern states, where slavery was generally not practiced. Regionally, this caused American life along the Ohio to move along two separate, unequal tracks of development and progress.

These two economic systems were noted by Alexis de Tocqueville, a French political writer, during a visit to the United States between 1831 and 1832. While traveling down the Ohio River, he made note of the differences between life in Ohio, where slavery did not exist, and in the slave state of Kentucky:

> These two states differ only in a single respect: Kentucky has admitted slavery, but the state of Ohio has prohibited the existence of slaves within its borders. Thus the traveler who floats down the current of the Ohio to the spot where that river falls into the Mississippi may be said to sail between liberty and servitude. . . . Upon the left bank of the stream the population is sparse; from time to time one [sees] a troop of slaves loitering in the half-desert fields; the primeval forest reappears at every turn; society seems to be asleep, man to be idle. . . . From the right bank, on the contrary, a confused hum is heard, which proclaims afar the presence of industry; the fields are covered with abundant harvests; the elegance of the dwellings announces the taste of activity of the laborers; and man appears to be in the enjoyment of that wealth and contentment which is the reward of labor. . . . Upon the left bank of the Ohio labor is confounded with the idea of slavery, while upon the right bank it is identified with that of prosperity and improvement.[33]

Riverboats were commonplace on the Ohio River by the 1830s and 1840s, making the ports in cities like Cincinnati busy places. The use of steam power changed the face of the frontier, prompting population growth, urbanization, and economic development throughout the Ohio Valley.

Given its unique geographical status as a dividing line between the slave and free states, the Ohio River became, by the early nineteenth century, a goal for southern slaves who escaped to find freedom in the north. By as early as the years just after the War of 1812, several routes to freedom had been established along the Ohio River. By the 1840s, with the coming of the railroad to the trans-Appalachian region, the system of safe houses and escape routes from the south to the north became known as the Underground Railroad.

By the 1850s, several towns along the Ohio River were part of the Underground Railroad. An important slave escape route reached the river town of Marietta, where many antislavery westerners from New England lived. A second route reached Yellow Springs, Ohio, on the Little Miami River, and another ran from the Ohio north along the tributary of the Great Miami, where the states of Indiana and Ohio joined. Abolitionist sites for Underground

Railroad stations were also found at Richmond, Centreville, Franklin, Bloomington, and others. Several small communities supported the Underground Railroad on the Ohio River, but others did not. Cincinnati, for example, was not a popular location for slave runaways to pass through, because the city was closely connected with southern merchants and traders.

One of the key routes used by slaves escaping north was at Ripley, Ohio, just 50 miles upriver from Cincinnati. In 1828, a Presbyterian minister named John Rankin purchased 65 acres along the Ohio River near Ripley and began operating "the first station on the Underground Railroad."[34] From an upper window in his two-story house, Reverend Rankin placed a lantern to signal runaway slaves their way to freedom. Slaves soon began to refer to Rankin's home as Liberty Hill. Hundreds of slaves passed through the Rankin estate, and, by 1860, perhaps as many as 2,000 fugitive slaves had reached either Rankin's home or Ripley after having crossed the Ohio River.

When war finally came to the Ohio River Valley and the United States split North and South in the spring of 1861, the Ohio River served as a less significant line of division between the two geographical and political sides. All the states north of the river remained loyal to the United States. Slave-holding Kentucky, however, did not secede from the Union, and by 1863,the western portion of Virginia split off from the commonwealth and formed its own new state, West Virginia, which did not support the Confederacy throughout the war.

Kentucky faced serious loyalty problems during the Civil War. As a slave state that did not join with its fellow southern states, Kentucky was conflicted. (Perhaps an indicator of Kentucky's split personality during the war was the fact that both the U.S. president, Abraham Lincoln, and the president of the Confederate States, Jefferson Davis, were born in Kentucky.) In time, the state government declared itself neutral in the war and did not officially participate. Kentuckians did fight in the war, however, on both sides, and Kentucky did see its share of battles and skirmishes.

REVEREND RANKIN INSPIRES MRS. STOWE

Reverend John Rankin of Ripley, Ohio, may have been one of the most active agents on the Underground Railroad, helping thousands of blacks escape southern slavery. He also figures importantly in the writing of one of the most influential books of the pre-Civil War era, one that presented slavery to many northerners as they had never read of it before.

In the fall of 1834, representatives of the Cincinnati Presbyterian Synod held meetings in John Rankin's church. One of the delegates was a guest at Rankin's home, a minister named Lyman Beecher, originally from Boston, who had recently moved to Cincinnati. In Beecher's company was his daughter Harriet, who later remembered sitting on the lawn in front of the Rankin home, "gazing over the broad river [the Ohio] to the golden Kentucky hills."* Another minister and college professor, Calvin Stowe, was also one of Rankin's guests.

One evening during the Beechers' stay, Reverend Rankin told of a young slave woman who had escaped from a plantation in Kentucky and reached his home. It had been late winter, and the frozen Ohio River was beginning to thaw, causing the ice to break up. Despite the unstable condition of the river, the slave woman escaped with her infant child, intent on reaching the Rankin station. When she reached the banks of the Ohio, "the woman ran onto the black river. Slipping and falling on the melting ice, she floundered on, guided by the lone light on the hilltop."** Once she arrived at the Rankin home, she was rescued and her clothes were dried out near Rankin's kitchen stove before she was escorted to the next station on the Underground Railroad. By the next morning, the Ohio River ice had broken apart completely, causing the slave catchers pursuing the young woman to believe she had drowned crossing the river.

Harriet Beecher never forgot Rankin's story of a slave woman leaping from one ice mass to another across the Ohio River. In the years that followed, she married Professor Stowe, and, in 1851, she wrote one of the most popular novels of the nineteenth century, a story of slavery titled *Uncle Tom's Cabin*. The book became a runaway bestseller. In her novel, Stowe presented sympathetic portraits of southern slaves, including a fictional slave character named Eliza Harris, who escaped, reached the Ohio River, and made a "midnight crossing of the ice-strewn river."*** It was a scene from real life that became one of the most remembered fictional scenes of American literature.

* Quoted in Havighurst, *River to the West,* 243.
** Ibid.
*** Ibid.

That summer, Union gunboats were gathered on the Ohio River and a federal campaign to deliver Union troops up two of the Ohio's main tributary arteries—the Tennessee and the Cumberland Rivers—was soon underway. By the early months of 1862, Union action was taking place elsewhere in the region, involving a federal commander who would one day become the North's greatest general of the war: Ulysses S. Grant. The Illinois general already had captured the Ohio River town of Paducah, in western Kentucky, on September 6, 1861. That evening, Grant returned by Ohio steamer to Cairo, Illinois, to begin his campaign to remove Confederate positions on the Tennessee and the Cumberland.

Confederate president Jefferson Davis sent one of his most experienced commanders, General Albert Sidney Johnston, to establish defenses stretching across the state, with Bowling Green, Kentucky, as his personal headquarters. Meanwhile, Union commanders Henry Halleck and Brigadier General Don Carlos Buell, who led the federal Army of the Ohio, were pressed to ensure control of Kentucky.

It was Buell who saw action first against Confederate forces at Mill Springs, Kentucky, on January 19. Near a site called Logan's Cross-Roads, one of Halleck's subordinates, General George Thomas, defeated the Confederates, killing one of their generals, Felix J. Zollicoffer. The rebel general, while fighting the battle in a pouring rain, became disoriented. As he rode between the battle lines wearing a white rubber raincoat, he mistook a Union colonel for a subordinate of his own. As he gave his enemy an order, the officer shot and killed Zollicoffer as he stood next to him. (Union troops later removed hairs from the dead Confederate's beard as souvenirs.)

The Union victory at Mill Springs helped Union forces hold onto eastern Kentucky. Western Kentucky continued to present a problem for the Federals (the Union forces). The Tennessee and Cumberland Rivers could provide an invasion route for the North into the region, as well as into Tennessee, but the

South had erected defensive forts, making access to these rivers, as well as to the Mississippi, difficult. Confederates had fortified Island No. 10 in the Mississippi, blocking northern river traffic south. They had also built Fort Henry on the Tennessee and Fort Donelson on the Cumberland. The two forts were erected just 12 miles from one another where the two rivers flowed close together.

Under Halleck's command, General Ulysses S. Grant, a lackluster West Point graduate who had only recently been recommissioned into the federal army, captured the outlets of both rivers into the Ohio River at Paducah and Smithland. By early February, Grant began his approach on Forts Henry and Donelson. His 15,000 men moved by steamboat up the two rivers. Flag Officer Andrew H. Foote commanded the river vessels, which included seven gunboats: four ironclads and three wooden.

On February 6, the gunboats began shelling Fort Henry. The fort was quickly abandoned by its Confederate occupants. (The facility was partially underwater at the time, given its low position near the river.) Grant followed, marching his men across the short distance to Fort Donelson while Foote dispatched his boats down the Tennessee, then up the Cumberland to meet Grant more than a week later.

Trapped by Union forces, the Confederate officers in the fort spent the night of February 15 to 16 deciding whether to fight or surrender. They chose surrender. Two officers turned their commands over to subordinates rather than taking responsibility for the surrender. It fell to General Simon Bolivar Buckner to deliver 13,000 Confederate troops into Grant's hands (more than 2,000 had already escaped the Union army).

When Buckner sent a messenger to request the terms of the surrender, Grant replied, "No terms except an unconditional and immediate surrender can be accepted. I propose to move immediately upon your works." The words would become immortal for Grant, who would often be referred to in the future as U.S. (Unconditional Surrender) Grant. With the fall

Because it formed the longest boundary between slaveholding states and free states, the Ohio River played an important part in the Civil War. Several battles were fought near the Ohio in Kentucky, a slave state that chose to remain neutral in the war. General Kirby Smith, seen here, was one Confederate general who fought in the area, capturing Lexington, Kentucky, and establishing a pro-southern state government.

of two Confederate forts, the Union had gained control of the Tennessee and Cumberland Rivers, which gave them access to the heartlands of the Confederacy. When Buckner surrendered to Grant, it was a reunion of sorts. The two men had been roommates at West Point.

With the removal of the Confederate forts, the Union was better able to control the region of the lower Ohio River

Valley. Historian R.E. Banta explains the significance the river gained in support of the northern war effort:

> The Ohio River was established as the chief and safest artery of supply and transport for the Union forces west of the [Appalachian] Mountains; its towns became the shipping points and depots for munitions and provisions and its boat-yards built gunboats from the keel up—including James B. Eads's first federal ironclads—and reconditioned and armed the purchased or captured river packets by the score.[35]

With northern states flanking its northern banks and neutral Kentucky to its south, the Ohio River enjoyed an insular position geographically, never witnessing any major combat throughout the war. However, the Ohio River region was the scene of several Confederate troop movements.

By the fall of 1862, central Kentucky, as well as the river towns of Louisville and Cincinnati, were threatened by the advance of a pair of Confederate armies under the commands of Generals Kirby Smith and Braxton Bragg. Smith approached from the east, having passed through the Cumberland Gap of the Appalachians, and Bragg had moved up from his positions south of Bowling Green, Kentucky. Smith's army captured Lexington, Kentucky, where it was later joined by General Bragg's forces. Together, the two Confederate leaders established a prosouthern state government, which was never officially recognized by the citizens of Kentucky.

Soon, Union General Don Carlos Buell delivered an army to central Kentucky to drive Bragg from Lexington. He had chased Bragg up from Tennessee; arrived at Louisville, where he received several steamboat loads of Union troops; and then ordered his enlarged army to split and move down the Tennessee River and east up the Ohio toward Lexington. Buell was able to place his forces between Bragg's Confederates and the Ohio River. They engaged each other in battle at Perryville, Kentucky, on October 8. During the four-hour battle, 7,000 men were killed or wounded. Although the battle was not decisively won or lost by either side, Bragg believed that his campaign in Kentucky had been stymied, and he and General Smith soon withdrew their forces from Kentucky back south into Tennessee. The battle at Perryville proved to be the last major engagement in the lower Ohio River Valley for the remainder of the war.

Confederate raiders continued to plague Union supporters in the region. Most of those raids were led by a flamboyant Confederate general named John Hunt Morgan. Morgan had been raised in Lexington, Kentucky. A veteran of the Mexican War, he raised a group of southern sympathizers, many of them native Kentuckians, and joined a regiment under the command of Simon Bolivar Buckner. Although Morgan's men began as infantry troops, they later gained their fame as horse-mounted infantry.

> Morgan saw action while attached to General Bragg's campaign in Kentucky. He and his men carried out dashing raids in advance of Bragg's often slow-moving troops. General Morgan's men moved with great speed and mobility as they traveled with nothing but arms and saddlebags, living on the country, dividing, reassembling, shadow boxing and feinting, stealing horses as they went, and indulging in tomfoolery which included the sending of telegraphic commands and fictitious reports of their position and objects to Union officers and assessing a levy of both pies and cash against captured towns. In addition they accumulated silver plate and jewelry for the benefit of the Confederate cause.[36]

"Morgan's Raiders" became so brazen in their raids that they began to raise a general fear among northern towns in the Ohio Valley region including those north of the Ohio River.

On July 7, 1863, General Morgan did, indeed, take his men across the Ohio from Brandenburg, Kentucky, into northern territory, delivering them onboard a pair of stolen steamboats. During the crossing, there was a brief exchange of gunfire with a Union gunboat which "fired a few shots, said it was out of ammunition, and left."[37] When Morgan reached the opposite bank, he and his men burned one of the steamboats.

With 2,000 men under his command, he moved across southern Indiana and Ohio on a five-day raid, burning buildings, stealing money and horses, and destroying rail lines. They landed at Mauckport, Indiana, and rode straight for the former state capital at Corydon. Facing little opposition from the Indiana Home Guard, Morgan's men stole horses and food. Morgan then extracted extortion money from the town's merchants and businessmen, collecting as much as $1,000 from each of them to guarantee he would not burn their businesses. After this raid, Morgan took his men northeast toward the towns of Salem, Scottsburg, Vernon, and Versailles. The local Home Guard units were unable to stop Morgan's advancing raid. (One legend tells of a local Home Guard commander who mistook Morgan's men for Union troopers and actually stopped the Confederate irregular commander to ask him of Morgan's whereabouts!) Morgan eventually rode his men into Ohio, where he raided the town of Harrison and then moved south to avoid Cincinnati, his intentions being to cross the Ohio into West Virginia. Along the banks of the river, near Buffington's Island, Union cavalry units caught up with Morgan and, after an overnight battle, captured the elusive Confederate raider. He later was placed in an Ohio prison. Morgan was not out of the picture for long. He eventually escaped, returned to his native Kentucky, and took up his raiding tactics again until he was finally killed during a raid in Tennessee in 1864.

That same summer of 1864 marked the last major conflict between Confederate and Federal troops on the Ohio River. The Mississippi had already fallen under Union control the previous year following General Grant's capture of Vicksburg, Mississippi, the last major Confederate stronghold on the southern-flowing river. By 1864, the southern states had clearly lost the war, and little action occurred in Kentucky. During the final year of the war, Union river traffic could make a complete trip up the Mississippi and the Ohio Rivers without any significant degree of threat.

6

A River in Transition

During the heyday of the steamboat era—the 1840s and 1850s—life in the Ohio River Valley became more commercialized, more urbanized, and more settled in general. However, the same could not immediately be said of the Ohio River itself. The inland rivers of America during the nineteenth century were largely untamed natural waterways, whose courses changed and shifted with their heavy, often swift currents, causing the rivers to recreate themselves constantly. Obstacles and barriers, largely natural, made river traffic on the Ohio River often hazardous, sometimes dangerous. During the 1800s, improvements were attempted on the river to create a more manageable, safer water route. As early as 1824, Congress, aware of the value of the Ohio as a route for western pioneers, appropriated $75,000 for river projects on both the Ohio and Mississippi Rivers. On May 24, 1824, Congress passed an act making the Corps of Engineers of the United States Army responsible for clearing the Ohio and keeping its course maintained, as well as its depth. Under the original mandate issued by Congress, the Corps of Engineers was to remove "planters, sawyers and snags" from the main channel of the Ohio River. The Corps uprooted stumps from the riverbed and constructed artificial banks for the river in an effort to force the river's waters to clear out menacing sand bars. For the next 20 years, additional money was earmarked annually for such river-related improvements.

In the mid-1840s, President James K. Polk declared such bills unconstitutional and little was done by the federal government to improve the condition of the Ohio and other western rivers until after the Civil War. Throughout the remainder of the nineteenth century, federal funds were appropriated and used to make river improvements, but the traffic on the river continued to decline, generally because of the competition provided by railroads.

Of the natural challenges presented by the historical Ohio River, none was considered greater than the Falls of the Ohio, situated near Louisville, Kentucky. The falls were more properly rapids, because the river fell 22 feet in two miles. The real problem presented by the Falls was the shallowness of the river.

Historian R.E. Banta describes the challenge of the Falls to river traffic:

> The river, in the state in which it existed when it was first thoroughly surveyed, had available for navigation over its worst shoals at lowest water a minimum of only one foot in places above Louisville; even below that city there were minimums of only two feet. The flow of water at the Falls themselves could, in extreme drought, be reduced to a trickle between the serrated rocks. In the river's natural state it was only when a minimum of three feet of water maintained over the worst shoals above and below the Falls that it was considered to be at a navigable stage for steamboats or other river craft of cargo size.[38]

With the advent of the steamboat era by the 1820s, the problem of the Falls needed a solution. In 1825, the Louisville and Portland Canal Company was created by investors from Kentucky and, over the next five years, a canal was built allowing boats to bypass the Falls completely. It opened for business in 1830, taking its first customer, the steamboat *Uncas*. The canal was two miles in length and featured three locks, each allowing boats up to 183 feet in length. By the 1870s, the lock compartments were increased in size to accommodate riverboats more than 300 feet long. Even though the canal was an immediate success, it faced such challenges as mud deposits and floodwaters carrying great floating trees.

In 1875, a new effort was begun to create yet another change in the course of the Ohio River. That year, after a survey of the river, plans were developed to create a six-foot-deep channel along the entire length of the Ohio, through the construction of control dams. Sixty-eight such dams were proposed, spanning the nearly 1,000 miles of the river. One of these dams was built at Davis Island, just five miles downriver from Pittsburgh, and completed in 1885. The project proved a success because "Pittsburgh had ample harbor space even during low water."[39]

The Davis Island Dam allowed Pittsburgh to harbor as many as 12,000 steamboats and barges.

However, additional construction of the multidam project took place slowly. Many people viewed such projects as unnecessary, because river traffic on the Ohio had trickled down to almost nothing, replaced by the ever-expanding railroads. "What's the good of a river with all these railroads?" was a common question on the river.[40] By 1929, more than 50 years after the project began, only 48 dams had been built.

The question of decreasing transportation on the Ohio River was an important one. After the Civil War (and, in part, because of the war), Ohio River traffic became almost nonexistent. Railroads replaced riverboats in the transportation of everything from passengers to freight. What river traffic remained was less about steamboats and more about fleets of barges pushed up and down the river by stern-wheel towboats. Coal towboats did remain one of the constant sights on the river, even during the latter decades of the nineteenth century. Steamboat traffic did not fade away entirely, even during the 1870s and 1880s. Those decades actually witnessed a short-lived resurgence of steamboating, "with as many as a million passengers and two and a half million tons of freight loaded in twelve months."[41]

The early twentieth century brought another decline in Ohio River traffic. Railroads continued to take their toll on the levels of commercial traffic on the Ohio. Little was being done to improve the general condition and navigability of the river which had been "left to the shantyboat people" who "like gypsies they came into town, raiding gardens, hencoops, and smoke houses, asking at the kitchen door for knives and scissors to grind. When they moved on, the river was empty."[42] River traffic during this period shrank to nearly nothing. Older steamboats sat at their moorings, serving little commercial purpose, except as floating taverns, dance halls, and gambling houses. During the winter of 1918, a great ice floe destroyed many of these relics of a more bustling river era. By that time, Ohio River cargo tonnage hit a new low of 4.6 million tons.

As the United States entered World War I in 1917, the river began to experience a new era of commercial traffic. By the spring of 1918, with the country's rail system unable to keep pace with the needed shipments of wartime materials, the Ohio and other inland waterways were pressed again into duty. Millions of tons of supplies, food, petroleum products, and other goods were soon being shipped down the Ohio River to New Orleans. Historian Walter Havighurst describes the wartime renaissance of the Ohio's commercial traffic:

> In [the] crisis the War Department rediscovered the rivers. One towboat could do the work of a dozen locomotives; a string of barges could carry the freight of hundreds of railroad cars. Rounding up all the tonnage that would float, recalling veteran pilots from retirement, and building new towboats and barges, the government formed the Federal Barge Lines. The forgotten rivers carried the commerce of war.[43]

After the war, attention remained focused on the Ohio River. The American rail system of the 1920s was aging, and producers, shippers, and exporters realized that a towboat on the Ohio could move barges loaded with commodities such as coal cheaper than the railroads could and just about as quickly. The Transportation Act of 1920 ensured that rivers such as the Ohio would remain open to heavy commercial use "while channels and terminals were improved and modernized." Four years later, the Federal Barge Lines, which had been created as a government entity, was privatized, making way for the Inland Waterways Corporation, "which opened the way for private carriers on the river."[44] Between 1922 and 1923, Congress appropriated nearly $100 million through the War Department to improve America's inland waterways and harbors, including the Ohio system. In 1923 alone, Congress appropriated almost $60 million to complete the work on 19 dams required to create a minimum nine-foot navigable channel on the Ohio from Pittsburgh to Cairo, Illinois. The locks built along these river dams were to measure a minimum of 600 feet in length and 110 feet in width. From 1923 through 1925, river traffic cargo tonnage nearly doubled from 10 million tons to 19 million.

Similarly, the 1920s witnessed the completion of the canalization of the Ohio River. By the end of the decade, 48 dams along the river had been constructed and the river had been channelized to a depth of nine feet. With the completion of this long-term river control project, "the river became a flight of water steps, through locks and dams, from Pittsburgh to Cairo."[45] These improvements in the navigability of the Ohio had a profound impact on the Ohio Valley and the commercial development of the river in the twentieth century. As the president of one Ohio River barge company put it:

> As the work of developing the network of channels progressed, commerce and industry came again to the rivers, slowly and hesitantly at first, then with increasing enthusiasm as the efficiency and dependability of the new barge transport was demonstrated. This rush of industry to the inland waterways has been particularly pronounced since World War II.[46]

By 1929, with a largely tamed and channeled river completed, Ohio River commerce amounted to 21 million tons of freight. Throughout the 1930s and the following decades, the Ohio River continued to see heavy traffic, remaining a key river of commerce. The modern towboat came into extensive use during the Great Depression and even more so during World War II "with the introduction of the diesel engine and replacement of the sternwheel by the screw propeller."[47] During the early 1940s, as the United States entered World War II, the Ohio River Valley played a strategic role in the domestic war effort. The river served two general purposes during the war, including the transportation of strategic materials and encouraging the "growth of manufacturing processes that normally would have been forced into congested coastal areas."[48] One key element of the Ohio River's wartime contribution was in the shipping of petroleum products. Because of the threat posed by German submarines along the American east coast, tankers on the Ohio came under the service of the U.S. Navy and "fleets of oil barges . . . were towed upstream to refineries on the Ohio River. Inland cities such as Pittsburgh . . . became supply instead of receiving points for these products."[49] Other strategic commodities of war, including barges filled with sulfur to be used in the manufacture of explosives, were towed up from the Mississippi River to the Ohio and to Ohio Valley factories and munitions plants. Naval vessels including landing craft and many ocean-going vessels, especially those with a draft of less than nine feet, were built in factories and ports along the Ohio River. In all, approximately 1,000 wartime vessels were constructed inland and shipped down the Ohio River to be used in the various theaters of war. Ohio River freight reached 36 million tons (1941) and more than 38 million tons by the following year. By the end of the war, the level of commercial traffic on the Ohio was reduced, but only temporarily. By 1947, freight weight surpassed 41 million tons.

Despite the recovery of the Ohio River, its commerce, and trade traffic following World War I, the river experienced some major challenges offered by nature itself. Even though the river had been channelized, dammed, and otherwise tamed through extensive efforts by the Army Corps of Engineers during the 1920s, a major flood wrecked havoc on those living along its banks in 1937.

The river had always experienced its ups and downs. A traveler to the Ohio Country in the spring of 1765 noted how a flood on the Ohio had destroyed the site of the Indian settlement known as Lower Shawnee Town, "which was all carried away, except 3 or 4 houses . . . [and] obliged the whole town to take to their canoes and move . . . to the hills."[50] A few years later, during the early 1770s, the river flooded again and "swept more than 100 feet of water past the site of Cincinnati."[51] The famous American painter and naturalist James Audubon wrote in his journal of a flood he witnessed along the river in the early 1800s, during which he observed "a cow swimming through the lower window of a house while the family huddles on the upper floor."[52] Every generation of those living along the river or within its broad bottomlands experienced an Ohio flood. There were serious inundations in 1847, 1884, and 1913.

Such floods caused the Ohio River to overflow its banks and distribute floodwaters across thousands of square miles of bottomland, covering all the buildings in the region under its muddy currents. Sometimes these raging floods even ripped buildings off their foundations and delivered them downstream.

In 1937, those living along the river experienced the greatest Ohio flooding in the river's recorded history. The rains came in with the New Year—falling heavily on January 2—scattered up and down the full length of the river, from Pittsburgh to Cairo. For a solid week, the rains came, steadily raising the Ohio's waters until the river overflowed its dams. At the end of the week, the rains slacked off, but the tributary streams of the Ohio—the Kentucky, Tennessee, Wabash, Big and Little Miamis, and Licking—were all swollen to capacity, sending floodwaters across bottomlands and delivering their heightened currents into the Ohio itself. Ten days after the rains began, the Ohio was at flood stage. South of Louisville, Kentucky, the rain-fed river sloshed over its banks, inundating hundreds of square miles of lowlands. Historian Walter Havighurst describes what followed:

> Then came new rains—thirty hours of downpour at Pittsburgh, a steady soaking across the middle valley. Highways and railways disappeared under muddy water. Thousands of lowland families began moving to higher ground. In Chicago the Coast Guard loaded surf boats on railroad cars for water-logged cities in southern Indiana. At the mouth of the Licking the river surged into sixty blocks of Newport, Kentucky. Cincinnati's basin streets were buried, and the Ohio backed up for miles into the populous Mill Creek Valley.[53]

At Cincinnati, the normal river level was 26 feet; twice that depth was considered flood stage. At times, the rains turned to snow, blanketing the landscape. Buildings were submerged under a

LOUISVILLE RECOVERS FROM THE FLOOD OF '37

Louisville, Kentucky, one of the largest cities along the Ohio River, experienced some of the worst flooding during the great 1937 inundation. Three-quarters of the city was flooded, 175,000 citizens were evacuated, and property damage estimates reached $50 million. After nearly three weeks of rain, the city's schools closed and remained so for another three weeks. The city went without electrical power for days, and boats patrolled the city's flooded streets, desperately searching for those trapped by the high waters. In all, more than 50,000 victims were rescued.

When the waters receded, Louisville valiantly struggled back to normality, as "every household and establishment underwent the arduous process of drying out, cleaning up, and resuming normal operation."* When one of its schools—Shawnee High School—was found to be unusable, students were farmed out to other schools. The girls in the senior class became involved in a cathartic writing project, which included collecting two dozen firsthand interviews of several of the city's flood victims.

Although many of Louisville's postflood problems were those experienced by towns and cities up and down the river, some were unique. At the Louisville Free Public Library, 25,000 books were collected, all water-soaked and slimy with mud. They were boxed up and shipped to Philadelphia to be dried out. In the library basement, the remains of the Louisville Museum of Science and Industry lay in ruins. Historian Walter Havighurst describes the museum mess:

tide of river water. Trains brought in over a dozen Navy surfboats. The new train terminal in Cincinnati became surrounded by water. Telephone service was cut, and city water service became sporadic. A church building floated down the river, its steeple bell pealing out a belated warning. Oil tanks "broke loose, spilling a million tons of gasoline."[54] In one day—January 22—the Ohio rose nearly seven feet. The river rose to a height of 60 feet, then 70 feet, until it crested at just over 80 feet, "8 feet higher than the previous record set in 1884."[55]

> In a muddy chaos lay the menagerie of mounted animals, a famous collection of birds, the bones of mastodon and mammoth, a whale skull, 20,000 mineral specimens, 5,000 sea shells, hundreds of Indian artifacts, 40 dioramas, and the mummy of an Egyptian princess. From that figure workers unwound 2,000 yards of soggy wrappings; it was dried in the big oven of the Louisville Gas and Electric Company and restored to the leathery body. For weeks the staff washed, rinsed, and dried thousands of wild life specimens.**

The people of Louisville proved to be made of valiant stuff after the flood, but perhaps most indicative of the city's unconquerable spirit was their determination to host their annual horseracing event, the Kentucky Derby. Although floodwaters had reached the horse track at Churchill Downs and turned it into a "lake of mud," (284), by early May, the track had been cleaned up, and the Derby was held, just as it had been every year since 1875, with 70,000 spectators in attendance.

Just as the high spirits and determination of the people of Louisville helped them recover from the flood, so did their sense of humor. Over at the Brown Hotel in downtown Louisville, a trophy of the flood was hung over the registration desk: a large river carp that one of the hotel's bellboys had caught in his hands as the flood current floated three feet deep through the hotel's lobby.

* Quoted in Havighurst, *River to the West*, 283.

** Ibid., 284.

All up and down the river, the floodwaters destroyed everything in their path. In Evansville, Indiana, 36,000 people lost their homes. In Moscow, Ohio, along the river and southeast of Cincinnati, more than 80 of the town's 90 homes were destroyed. Just downstream, at New Richmond, Ohio, the waters ripped 200 homes off their footings and sent 50 of them down river. In Paducah, Kentucky, those staying at the Irvin S. Cobb Hotel took to the high ground of the hotel's mezzanine balcony as nine feet of water flooded the main floor. The guests remained trapped

In the early twentieth century, the Army Corps of Engineers worked to tame the Ohio River. However, they could not control the frequent floods that tormented the inhabitants of the Ohio River Valley. In this photograph, children float through flood waters along the Ohio in West Virginia.

until rescue boats were rowed into the hotel through the upper windows. As floodwaters engulfed 30 square miles of Louisville, Kentucky, the city's electric generating plant was flooded, shrouding the river community in darkness. From a downtown hotel, Western Union Telegraph operators moved to an upper story, hooked their telegraph sets up to tractor batteries and sent desperate messages to the outside world. One unfortunate towboat, the *Thomas Moses,* along with its two barges, was swept along the flood tide until it came to rest in a treetop five miles away from the river's previous channel.

After weeks of rains and flooding, the Ohio's current began to subside during the final days of January. During the following days, weeks, and even months, those who had experienced the worse flood along the Ohio in half a century began their recovery. Tens of thousands of stranded people were rescued from along the flooded waterways. Streets and buildings were cleaned, power was restored, and municipal water systems came back on line. Although little could be done to repair the psychological damage of the Flood of 1937, little by little, life along the Ohio River eventually returned to its former rhythms, just as the river returned to many of its former banks.

7

The Modern Ohio River

Today, the Ohio River is a waterway susceptible to spring floods, and major flood control systems remain in place to monitor the river's levels. In addition to earlier flood control systems, more modernized locks and dams have been built since 1955 to allow easier and faster transit of commercial barges, as well as leisurecraft and excursion boats. A canal (originally opened in 1830) remains in use at Louisville, and river traffic still bypasses the Falls of the Ohio, a series of rapids that cause the river to drop 24 feet over a river distance of just over two miles. With the increase of commercial traffic on the river after World War II, the U.S. Army Corps of Engineers correctly predicted, "the demands of industry will double the freight load."[56] Over the past 50 years, much of the original dam restraints on the Ohio River have been replaced with more modern adaptations. Great locks have been constructed to accommodate the ever-increasing dimensions of the towboat–barge traffic on the river. By the 1970s, the Ohio Waterway Project had become a billion-dollar program.

The reworking of the Ohio's water management system has undergone complete overhaul since the 1950s, and other river-related issues have repeatedly taken center stage. In more recent decades, more and more people have become concerned with the levels of pollution found in the Ohio. As early as 1948, eight states—including Illinois, Indiana, Kentucky, New York, Ohio, Pennsylvania, Virginia, and West Virginia—signed an agreement called the Ohio River Valley Sanitation Compact (ORSANCO). At the heart of the compact was the question of the river's future viability as a waterway that could serve as an industrial river and a source of recreation, including fishing, swimming, and pleasure boating. As one newspaper editor in Cincinnati described the interstate agreement, "This is a treaty . . . marking not the end of a war but the beginning of one—a concerted fight by eight states backed by the federal government to end the disgusting pollution of the Ohio and its tributaries."[57] By the mid-1950s, all eight states supporting the compact had created state control boards, legally defined sanitation standards, passed

The Ohio River is a busy commercial route, running through industrial centers like Cleveland, seen above. Unfortunately, over the years this has led to severe pollution in the river and along its banks, threatening many fish and wildlife species. In recent years, several states along with the Army Corps of Engineers have taken action to curtail pollution of the river.

water pollution laws, and placed much of the administration of the river into a small number of oversight agencies. Sewage plants were redesigned to lower the levels of wastewater entering the Ohio River. Such laws and renewed awareness of the fragility of the Ohio River have produced, over the past several decades, a river teeming with new life. As the writer John Ed Pearce notes, "The Ohio used to be filthy, but over the past thirty years the

Ohio River Sanitation Compact has done a good job of cleaning it up. You see a lot more people swimming along the shore than you did a decade ago, and the growing number of birds indicates more aquatic life."[58]

Less than a century ago, the river served as a limited commercial route, with only 5 million tons of cargo (1917) passing along its route. Today, commercial use of the Ohio River is booming, consisting of hundreds of millions of tons of cargo annually. In 1993, the amount of Ohio River barge commerce amounted to nearly 235 million tons, including oil, gasoline, grains, chemicals, and coal, as well as sand and gravel shipments. One towboat may ply its way down the river in command of low-riding barges with as much as 7 million gallons of gasoline and diesel fuel in their holds. Although most of the Ohio River commercial boats move their cargoes up and down the river, there is also a significant amount of cross-river traffic, because industries ship goods and commodities from one bank of the river to the other.

These modern commercial towboats are technological wonders of the river. Each tow has the capacity to push as many as a dozen barges upriver while the pilot constantly scans the river from his air-conditioned pilothouse perched on top of the diesel-powered tow, in much the same way nineteenth-century steamboat captains piloted the great wheel in their own Texas pilothouses. Piloting such barges takes great skill and experience. Barge runs vary in size, and some measure as large as 1,190 by 105 feet. As their pilots maneuver such immense barges into various locks on the river, some of which measure barely larger than the barges themselves, they are left with no margin of error.

This commercial traffic adds to the pollution worries facing the Ohio. Any river traffic, whether commercial or recreational, often stirs up the river sediments, blocking sunlight, and reducing the river's oxygen levels, making survival difficult for marine life, such as fish and mollusks. Also, commercial tankers and barges occasionally spill their contents, causing pollution. In January of 1988, the Ohio River experienced a significant oil spill just southeast of Pittsburgh, resulting in the contamination of downstream drinking water in several states. According to ORSANCO, the number of such spills has continued to increase since 1988.

Commercial barges and towboats continue to use the river extensively, but the Ohio River also has proven alluring for recreational use. In fact, recreational boats make up the majority of the boating use of the Ohio River. In 1993, for example, recreational boats accounted for 80 percent of the boating "pressure" on the Ohio. Nearly 500 public and private boating facilities and ramps dot the banks of the Ohio River, including almost 200 marinas. The era of the steam riverboats has long since passed, but modern riverboats, usually used for excursions on the river, carry 1 million passengers annually along the Ohio. Some of those large riverboats are floating casinos, which provide significant sources of revenue for many communities along the river.

Today, the Ohio River represents a waterway of conflict. Modern Americans utilize the river in contradictory ways, as a commercial artery, a recreation area, an industrial support, a source of drinking water, and a dumping ground. The river's ecosystem remains tenuous today as both natural changes in the river, as well as the human impact, have created a complex system based on a delicate balance.

Once a river that supported approximately 164 species of fish, 127 species and subspecies of freshwater mussels, and 36 species of water birds, the Ohio has lost much of this, with the numbers declining over the past 50 years, in part because of the loss of natural habitat caused by the man-made restructuring of the river's navigation system. The number of native freshwater mussels on the river, for example, including subspecies, has dropped to approximately 50 varieties. Several aquatic species have already become extinct, including the harelip sucker, scioto pigtoe, and the round cornshell clam. Dozens of mussel species and subspecies are today on the federal endangered list, as are eight fish species. By altering the river's natural channels and by cutting off the Ohio from its natural floodplain, areas that have been vital as fish and wildlife habitats have been reduced and sometimes completely

ZEBRA MUSSEL, AN UNINVITED GUEST

The modern Ohio River has seen a decline in the numbers and variety of its fish, wildlife, and mussel populations, but more recent years have witnessed the arrival of a mussel type new to—and unwanted in—the Ohio.

Zebra mussels began invading several of North America's waterways during the 1980s and 1990s. They had reached the Ohio River by 1991. Zebra mussels are native to such European waters as the Caspian and Black Seas. Ocean vessels in that region unknowingly picked up zebra mussels on their hulls and transported them to the Great Lakes and other adjacent waterways, including the Ohio.

Although the foreign mussels are usually no larger than a human fingernail, they have caused hundreds of millions of dollars of damage to America's water systems and industrial plants, massing in such large numbers they are able to clog water intakes and water delivery systems.

The zebra mussels are also considered a threat to America's domestic mussel populations. Freshwater mussels on the Ohio and its tributaries are pushed out of their native habitats by the zebras, which have the ability to attach themselves to any solid surface, including the shells of the domestic freshwater mussels.

Since the mid-1990s, a concerted effort by federal, state, and private entities has been at work on limiting the expanding zebra mussel population and their destruction of both man-made facilities and natural habitats, but the pesky, immigrant mussels from half way around the world have proven difficult to reduce in numbers.

eliminated. The result has proven problematic for river wildlife and fish species:

> The original Ohio was characterized by a natural balance; sediment and silt may have filled a side channel, but a new side channel was created by the erosive power of flood waters. Particular islands and sandbars may have washed away, but new ones were built elsewhere by the river. The overall mosaic of the floodplain forest and wetlands, side channels and sloughs, islands and sandbars stayed more or less the same.

> However, in order to create a reliable and navigable river, the Ohio was transformed into a deep, fast-flowing canal. Consequentially, the river has been stripped of its ability to maintain itself—to carve new side channels, inundate its floodplain, and nourish and shelter the river wildlife.[59]

Countless generations of aquatic birds, such as ducks, geese, and others, have used the Ohio for breeding and nesting and as a food source, but the populations of such wildlife has decreased in more recent decades. Some experts and conservationists would like to see future floodplain management that would allow thousands of wing dams, and river-channel blocking facilities might be reworked to allow periodic flooding of river lowlands to provide additional "natural" habitat for future wildlife.

Currently, the U.S. Army Corps of Engineers is at work on an extensive program of habitat restoration as they work alongside several conservation organizations. The program, announced publicly in 2000, calls for a 15-year project designed to "restore side channels, islands, gravel spawning beds, and floodplain forests and wetlands without interfering with commercial navigation or other traditional river uses."[60] The Corps has worked closely with the United States Fish and Wildlife Service, as well as several state agencies and officials in each state bordering the Ohio River. Together, they have identified more than 300 potential habitat restoration project sites. Already, hundreds of millions of dollars have been spent on the extensive and well-intended restoration program.

As the Ohio River flows into the twenty-first century, the future of the river remains in question. How will the river survive the demands of an increasing river-based population? How can the delicate ecology of the river be maintained? How can the river be shared by all of its constituencies without resulting in the destruction of the river itself? Such difficult questions will demand thoughtful answers and decisive actions on the part of federal, state, and local entities in the decades to come.

Millions of dollars have been spent on restoration programs for the Ohio River, hoping to help the river and its inhabitants flourish and coexist with industry, and continue to be a source of beauty, recreation, and commerce.

Although the future of the river remains for another generation to address, one thing remains clear: The mighty Ohio River, carrying the waters of dozens of tributary streams, has helped create and form America's past. As generations of Americans have rolled across its fertile fields, hardwood forests, and urban landscapes, the river flows on, in the words of writer John Ed Pearce, with "waters that sprang from the plains near Lake Erie and surged through the hills of North Carolina and West Virginia, that carried tows and barges, bass boats and water skiers, dredges and excursion boats, that cooled the steel and turned the turbines of a hundred plants, flowing down through the heartland of America."[61]

5000 B.C. Native Americans in the Ohio River Valley have established hunting societies, track big game using stone-tipped spears, and work with copper, creating spearheads, axes, knives, awls and wedges.

500 B.C.–A.D. 500 The earliest mound-building Native American culture, the Adena, build burial sites for their dead, including mounds in the shapes of animals, such as frogs, bears, and birds.

A.D. 500–700 The Hopewellian Culture of mound-building peoples along the Ohio River Valley exists.

1000–1600 The Effigy Mound Culture of Native Americans in the Ohio Country, located in southern Wisconsin and Ohio exists.

1662 A French Jesuit priest, Father Lalemant, records information gathered from the Iroquois concerning the location of the Ohio River.

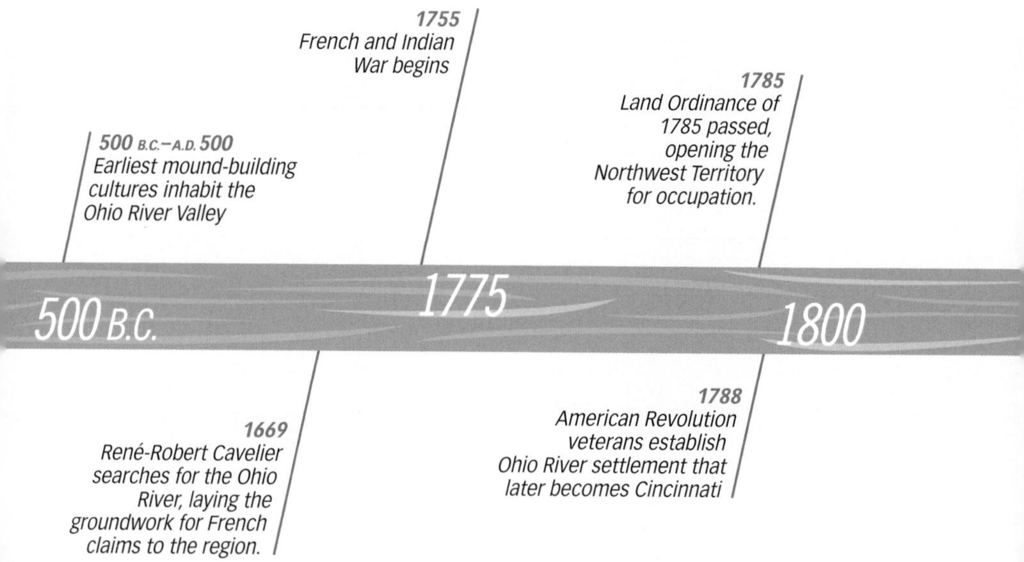

500 B.C.–A.D. 500
Earliest mound-building cultures inhabit the Ohio River Valley
1755
French and Indian War begins
1785
Land Ordinance of 1785 passed, opening the Northwest Territory for occupation.
500 B.C.
1775
1800
1669
René-Robert Cavelier searches for the Ohio River, laying the groundwork for French claims to the region.
1788
American Revolution veterans establish Ohio River settlement that later becomes Cincinnati

1669 French explorer René-Robert Cavelier, Sieur de La Salle, searches for the Ohio River. His explorations help lay the groundwork for French claim to the Ohio Country.

1692 A Dutchman from New York, Arnout Viele, reaches the Ohio River and paddles with his party down the full length of the river to its mouth.

1700 English traders, led by French guide Jean Coutoure, reach the Ohio River, and sail downriver to the Mississippi.

1720 English explorer Alexander Spotswood maps the Ohio River for the governor of Virginia.

1744 Delegates from New York, Pennsylvania, Maryland, and Virginia colonies purchase a tract of the Ohio Country from the Iroquois.

1801 — *1900* — *2000*

1811–12
The first western steamboat, the New Orleans, travels down the Ohio from Pittsburgh to New Orleans

1824
Congress makes the U.S. Army Corps of Engineers responsible for clearing the Ohio and keeping its course and depth maintained

1850
Top ten U.S. cities include three Ohio River towns: Pittsburgh, Cincinnati, and Louisville

1920
The Transportation Act ensures the Ohio will remain open to heavy commercial use

1937
Ohio River faces its worst flooding in recorded history

1993
Ohio River barge commerce reaches 235 tons

1747 The Ohio Company of Virginia receives a royal grant of 500,000 acres of Ohio for colonization and settlement.

1749 The governor of New France dispatches Pierre Joseph de Celoron de Bienville into the Ohio Country to make a French claim to the region.

1754 Irish-born frontiersman Christopher Gist accompanies young George Washington into the Ohio Country to warn the French out of the region.

1755 The French and Indian War to determine whether the British or French will dominate the Ohio River Valley begins.

1763 The Treaty of Paris ends the French and Indian War successfully for the British, who close the trans-Appalachian Ohio Country to further white settlement by issuing the Proclamation of 1763.

1777–79 Western frontiersman George Rogers Clark captures several key Ohio Valley forts from the British during the American Revolution. He and his party of Rangers float the Ohio River during the winter, surprising the British garrisons.

1785 The Articles of Confederation Congress passes the Land Ordinance of 1785, which opens the Ohio River Valley's Northwest Territory for occupation through land sales. The act calls for a survey of the region.

1787 The Articles of Confederation Congress passes the Northwest Ordinance of 1787, establishing a governmental system for the Old Northwest. That same year, General Rufus Putnam leads a group of pioneers to the Ohio River, where they established the settlement of Marietta, Ohio.

1788 American Revolution veterans establish the Ohio River settlement of Losantville, which is renamed Cincinnati two years later.

1791–94 The U.S. government engages in a war with Ohio Country tribes led by Chief Little Turtle. The Indians lose and are forced to surrender large tracts of land.

1792 The Ohio Country territory of Kentucky becomes the 15th state.

1796 The Ohio Country territory of Tennessee becomes the 16th state. That same year, President George Washington is authorized by Congress to contract with Ebenezer Zane to establish a trail into Ohio. The trail is later called Zane's Trace.

1801 The value of all trade gods shipped down the Ohio and its tributaries to New Orleans is $3.6 million.

1811–12 The first western steamboat, the *New Orleans,* completes a voyage down the Ohio from Pittsburgh to New Orleans.

1813–14 Henry Shreve and Daniel French build the first western steamboat (the *Enterprise*) to complete a voyage up the entire length of the Ohio River.

1824 Congress passes an act making the U.S. Army Corps of Engineers responsible for clearing the Ohio River and keeping its course maintained, as well as its depth.

1830 The Louisville and Portland Canal Company complete a canal that bypasses the Falls of the Ohio at Louisville, aiding river traffic.

1835 The first steamboat packet service (regularly scheduled arrivals and departures) reaches the Ohio River.

1847 This is the busiest year for flatboats on the Ohio River, with more than 2,600 making the trip from the Ohio River to New Orleans.

1850 The top ten cities in the United States include three Ohio River towns: Cincinnati, Pittsburgh, and Louisville.

1851 American writer Harriet Beecher Stowe publishes her popular novel *Uncle Tom's Cabin*, set in the slave world of Kentucky. One of her characters, Eliza Harris, an escaped slave, is portrayed crossing the Ohio River to freedom in the north.

1850s Railroads begin to replace the steamboats as the primary transportation for delivering cargo and passengers to the Ohio River Valley.

1862 General Grant captures two Confederate forts on the Tennessee and Cumberland Rivers, two major tributaries of the Ohio River. That same year, Confederate armies threaten the Ohio River towns of Louisville and Cincinnati.

1863 "Morgan's Raiders" cross the Ohio River from Kentucky into Ohio and carry out a series of raids across the northern state. General Morgan is finally killed by Union troops in 1864.

1875 New effort is begun to create a six-foot-deep channel along the entire length of the Ohio River.

1885 Davis Island Dam is completed, allowing Pittsburgh to harbor as many as 12,000 steamboats and barges.

1900–1910 This decade is the low point for commercial traffic on the Ohio River.

1911 A reproduction of the first western steamboat, the *New Orleans,* is launched to mark the centennial of the first steamer on the Ohio.

1920 The Transportation Act ensures that rivers such as the Ohio would remain open to heavy commercial use "while channels and terminals were improved and modernized."

1923 During this single year, Congress appropriates nearly $60 million to complete the work on 19 dams required to create a minimum nine-foot navigable channel on the Ohio River. The project is largely completed by 1929.

1929 Forty-eight dams have been constructed to control the flow of the Ohio River.

1937 The Ohio River Valley faces its worst flooding in recorded history.

1940s The Ohio River is used extensively for the war effort as 1,000 wartime vessels are constructed inland and shipped down the Ohio River, along with tens of millions of tons of war-related cargo.

1948 Eight Ohio Valley states sign an agreement called the Ohio River Valley Sanitation Compact, designed to help maintain the waterway for commercial, industrial, and recreational use, and to control pollution.

1950s All eight Ohio Valley states create state control boards to define sanitation standards for the river, as well as water pollution laws.

1970s The Ohio Waterway Project is funded with more than $1 billion for programs.

1993 The amount of Ohio River barge commerce reaches nearly 235 million tons, including oil, gasoline, grains, chemicals, and coal, as well as sand and gravel shipments.

2000 U.S. Army Corps of Engineers announces a program to "restore side channels, islands, gravel spawning beds, and floodplain forests and wetlands to the Ohio River Valley."

NOTES

CHAPTER 1

1. Quoted in Walter Havighurst, *River to the West: Three Centuries of the Ohio* (New York: G.P. Putnam's Sons, 1970), 19–20.
2. Quoted in Betty Bryant, *Here Comes the Showboat!* (Lexington: The University Press of Kentucky, 1998), xi.
3. Quoted in R.E. Banta, *The Ohio* (New York: Rinehart & Company, 1949), 18.
4. Ibid., 23.
5. Ibid., 24

CHAPTER 2

6. Quoted Banta, *The Ohio,* 45.
7. Ibid., 50.
8. Quoted in Havighurst, *River to the West,* 19.
9. Quoted in Banta, *The Ohio,* 55.
10. Ibid., 56.

CHAPTER 3

11. Quoted in Banta, *The Ohio,* 61.
12. Ibid., 63.
13. Ibid., 65.
14. Ibid., 67.
15. Ibid., 88.
16. Ibid., 149.
17. Quoted in John Ed Pearce, *The Ohio River*. Lexington: The University Press of Kentucky, 1989, 39.
18. Quoted in Frederic Austin Ogg, *The Old Northwest: A Chronicle of the Ohio Valley and Beyond* (New York: United States Publishers Association, Inc., 1919), 99.
19. Ibid., 106.

CHAPTER 4

20. Quoted in Richard A. Bartlett, *The New Country: A Social History of the American Frontier, 1776–1890* (New York: Oxford University Press, 1974), 309.
21. Quoted in Federal Writers' Project of the WPA, *Kentucky: A Guide to the Bluegrass State* (New York: Harcourt, Brace and Company, republished 1973) (originally published in 1939), 337.
22. Quoted in Pearce, *The Ohio River,* 167.
23. Stephen Ambrose, and Douglas Brinkley, *The Mississippi and the Making of a Nation* (Washington, D.C.: National Geographic Society, 2002), 84–85.
24. Ibid., 85.
25. Quoted in Judith St. George, *The Amazing Voyage of the New Orleans* (New York: G.P. Putnam's Sons, 1980), 55.
26. Quoted in Ambrose, *The Mississippi,* 85.
27. Quoted in Norbury L. Wayman, *Life on the River: A Pictorial History of the Mississippi, the Missouri, and the Western River System* (New York: Bonanza Books, 1971), 144.
28. Edith McCall, *Conquering the Rivers: Henry Miller Shreve and the Navigation of America's Inland Waterways* (Baton Rouge: Louisiana State University Press, 1984), 134.
29. *Niles' Weekly Register,* 1 July 1815.
30. Quoted in Richard C. Wade, *The Urban Frontier: The Rise of Western Cities, 1790–1830* (Cambridge: Harvard University Press, 1967), 39.
31. Ibid., 44.
32. Ibid.

CHAPTER 5

33. *http://xroads.virginia.edu-HYPER/DETOC/1ch18.html*
34. Quoted in Havighurst, *River to the West,* 241.
35. Quoted in Banta, *The Ohio,* 473.
36. Ibid., 475.
37. Quoted in Pearce, *The Ohio River,* 153.

CHAPTER 6

38. Quoted in R.E. Banta, *The Ohio,* 510.
39. Ibid., 512.

40. Ibid.
41. Ibid., 513.
42. Quoted in Havighurst, *River to the West,* 256–57.
43. Ibid., 256.
44. Ibid.
45. Quoted in Wayman, *Life on the River,* 315.
46. Ibid., 316.
47. Ibid.
48. Quoted in Banta, *The Ohio,* 519.
49. Ibid.
50. Quoted in Havighurst, *River to the West,* 278.
51. Ibid.
52. Ibid.
53. Ibid., 279.
54. Ibid., 280.
55. Ibid.

CHAPTER 7

56. Quoted in Havighurst, *River to the West,* 259.
57. Ibid., 288.
58. Quoted in Pearce, *The Ohio River,* 14.
59. Note to be supplied by author
60. *http://www.americanrivers.org/pressrelease/ohiopress8.3.00.html*
61. Quoted in Pearce, *The Ohio River,* 187.

Ambrose, Stephen and Douglas Brinkley. *The Mississippi and the Making of a Nation.* Washington, D.C.: National Geographic Society, 2002.

Banta, R.E. *The Ohio.* New York: Rinehart & Company, 1949.

Bartlett, Richard A. *The New Country: A Social History of the American Frontier, 1776–1890.* New York: Oxford University Press, 1974.

Bigham, Darrel E. *Towns & Villages of the Lower Ohio.* Lexington: The University Press of Kentucky, 1998.

Bryant, Betty. *Here Comes the Showboat!* Lexington: The University Press of Kentucky, 1994.

Federal Writers' Project of the WPA. *Kentucky: A Guide to the Bluegrass State.* New York: Harcourt, Brace and Company, republished 1973 (originally published in 1939).

Filson, John. *The Discovery and Settlement of Kentucke.* Ann Arbor: University Microfilms, Inc., 1966.

Gillespie, Michael. *Come Hell or High Water: A Lively History of Steamboating on the Mississippi and Ohio Rivers.* Stoddard, WI: Heritage Press, 2001.

Hagedorn, Ann. *Beyond the River: The Untold Story of the Heroes of the Underground Railroad.* New York: Simon & Schuster, 2002.

Havighurst, Walter. *River to the West: Three Centuries of the Ohio.* New York: G.P. Putnam's Sons, 1970.

Hurt, R. Douglas. *The Ohio Frontier: Crucible of the Old Northwest, 1720–1830.* Bloomington: Indiana University Press, 1996.

Josephy, Alvin M. *The Indian Heritage of America.* Boston: Houghton Mifflin Company, 1991.

McCall, Edith. *Conquering the Rivers: Henry Miller Shreve and the Navigation of America's Inland Waterways.* (Baton Rouge: Louisiana State University Press, 1984.

McConnell, Michael N. *A Country Between: The Upper Ohio Valley and Its People, 1724–1774.* Lincoln: University of Nebraska Press, 1992.

Merk, Frederick. *History of the Westward Movement.* New York: Alfred A. Knopf, 1980.

Niles Weekly Register, 1 July 1815.

Ogg, Frederic Austin. *The Old Northwest: A Chronicle of the Ohio Valley and Beyond.* New York: United States Publishers Association, Inc., 1919.

Parker, Sandra. *"Tecumseh" and Other Stories of the Ohio River Valley.* Bowling Green, OH: Bowling Green State University Popular Press, 2000.

Pearce, John Ed. *The Ohio River.* Lexington: The University Press of Kentucky, 1989.

Richter, Daniel K. *Facing East From Indian Country: A Native History of Early America.* Cambridge, MA: Harvard University Press, 2001.

Ryle, Russell G. *Ohio River Images: Cincinnati to Louisville in the Packet Boat Era.* Chicago: Arcadia Publishing, 2000.

St. George, Judith. *The Amazing Voyage of the New Orleans.* New York: G.P. Putnam's Sons, 1980.

Scheiber, Harry N., ed. *The Old Northwest.* Lincoln: University of Nebraska Press, 1969.

Skinner, Constance Lindsay. *Pioneers of the Old Southwest: A Chronicle of the Dark and Bloody Ground.* New York: United States Publishers Association, Inc., 1919.

Smith, Dwight L. and Ray Swick. *A Journey Through the West: Thomas Rodney's 1803 Journal from Delaware to the Mississippi Territory.* Athens: Ohio University Press, 1997.

Wade, Richard C. *The Urban Frontier: The Rise of Western Cities, 1790–1830.* Cambridge, MA: Harvard University Press, 1967.

Wayman, Norbury L. *Life on the River: A Pictorial History of the Mississippi, the Missouri, and the Western River System.* New York: Bonanza Books, 1971.

INDEX

page:
7: © CORBIS
14: © Hulton|Archive by Getty Images
25: © Hulton|Archive by Getty Images
30: Library of Congress
39: © Bettmann/CORBIS
51: © Archivo Iconografico, S.A./CORBIS
56: Library of Congress, LC-DIG-cwpb-06082
70: © Bettmann/CORBIS
74: © Charlie Borland/Index Stock Imagery
79: © Jeff Friedman/Index Stock Imagery

Frontis: Library of Congress Maps Division
Cover: © Roger Ressmeyer/CORBIS

ABOUT THE AUTHOR

TIM MCNEESE is an Associate Professor of History at York College in Nebraska. Professor McNeese earned an Associate of Arts degree from York College, a Bachelor of Arts degree in history and political science from Harding University, and a Master of Arts degree in history from Southwest Missouri State University. He is currently in his 28th year of teaching.

Professor McNeese's writing career has earned him a citation in the "Something About the Author" reference work. He is the author of more than sixty books and educational materials on everything from Egyptian pyramids to American Indians. He is married to Beverly McNeese, who teaches English at York College.